THE KINGDOM SYSTEM

The Correct Choice to the Alternative Systems of This World

CHARLIE LEWIS

The Kingdom System: The Correct Choice to the Alternative Systems of this World
by Charlie Lewis

Fedd Books
P.O. Box 341973
Austin, TX 78734

www.thefeddagency.com

Published in association with The Fedd Agency, Inc., a literary agency.

Cover Design: Christian Rafetto (www.humblebooksmedia.com)

ISBN: 9781957616896

LCCN: 2024910121

Printed in the United States of America

www.charlielewis.net

CONTENTS

INTRODUCTION

Crises have a way of revealing our priorities. Disease, broken relationships, job loss, and traumatic circumstances make the search an urgent one. In our quest for guidance and understanding of these situations for which current knowledge and past experiences are not enough, we often feel as though life is not working as it should. We feel confident that something must be available that will make a difference. At this fork in the road, we have two options: go down the path that leads to God's kingdom (a life in Jesus that is fully surrendered to Him, grace-giving, life-sustaining, and eternal) or choose the path of worldly sorrow (a life apart from His grace that leads to misery and destruction).

Then, there are those who love Jesus, but who are functionally living without His grace, direction, or power. They are dragging themselves through life without intimacy with the Father or a clear understanding of the governance and government of His kingdom. They follow the instructions of religion but miss the intimacy of relationship and lack an understanding of God's kingdom. At one point, that was me.

This is not a book about religion. This study was not motivated by religion, nor was it a religious search. I am a businessperson and an entrepreneur. My search was prompted by a desire to understand business better, not religion.

I define religion as man's attempt to explain communication with our Creator God through some type of method. That is why we have groups called Methodists, Baptists, Catholics, Pentecostals, Charismatics, and so on. I do not say that disparagingly or as if it is a diabolical plot. That is not the way it happened. A good experience, a good thought, a good idea became a doctrine, and huge denominations formed around either of those good things. The challenge is to build on the experience, thought, or idea without allowing it to be exclusive, divisive, and completely non-relational.

I grew up in Jacksonville, Florida to God-fearing, hard-working parents who were part owners of a small retail furniture chain and also oversaw a furniture manufacturing business. After returning from duty in Viet Nam as a pilot and airfield commander, God led me and my wife, Fran, to leave military life and return to the private sector. Over the past five decades, God has opened incredible doors for us. First, he opened doors in the furniture business, then—led by my wife—the jewelry business, and finally, the insurance industry.

I am not a pastor, but Fran and I—just like every believer in God's kingdom—are ministers of the Gospel. We made the decision before marriage to put God first: to pray then obey His direction. It was not easy, and at times, we did not know what the next step would be.

What we learned is that our Creator is a God of relationship. He is not religious (rules-based), nor is He capable of being defined by a single method. Religious people always have difficulty with relationship when they become too entrenched in their method. Have you ever worked with someone who values processes over people? Doing so is not life-giving, and it is rarely successful. The process of religion often defines rules but eliminates the need for relationship: "If you do tasks A, B, and C, you gain points." That's not Christianity.

Early on in life, I was a very religious person. Though it took some time, and God certainly had to put Fran and me through His "refiner's fire," we began to see what a non-religious type of relationship with God could look like. As I launched into a very tumultuous world (Viet Nam, protests, the hippie movement, etc.), I found that God was not confined to my box, nor were the situations, circumstances, and relationships I experienced. Essentially, the somewhat sheltered environment of my religion-based upbringing was put to the test. When real life and adulthood—going off to war as a newlywed, returning to start a business—arose, I found that the tools in my "religion box" did not serve me well.

Yes, I loved Jesus—but I had no idea that He wanted to play an active, intimate role in my everyday life. My faith was based on processes more than personal relationship: on instructions to follow more than an intimate relationship to enjoy and embrace. There were many times I found that regardless of how faithful I was in following those instructions, the answer for my situation, circumstance, or relationship was not in my religion. My experience did not produce results that aligned with the promises and descriptions found in the written Word. It was as if I had an understanding *of* God, but a stunted relationship *with* God.

Like the trained military pilot and airfield commander that I was, those religious years were like sitting in a cockpit with no fuel to fly the airplane. Yes, the plane was real, but it was grounded. It did not matter how many times I read the flight manual; I was not going anywhere. The fuel I needed to fly the plane—an intimate relationship with Jesus through a revelation of His kingdom—was absent.

Several years ago, I found myself in a very difficult business crisis (which I will share about later). Through its rather long process, I was driven into the written Word to find out what our Creator wanted to teach me. I discovered that I really did have a choice. There are two systems, and I could decide which system I wanted to live under. I could choose to believe the tangible circumstances I saw or to trust what God said. I could become a victim to what was happening to me or declare what I knew to be the truth according to God's Word.

It took me more than half a lifetime to realize that I had labored under the false belief that taking a "leap of faith" into God's kingdom was risky. Sure, I knew Jesus was important, but I believed that if you took it too far (i.e., tried to leave the world's system of laws and logic and live completely in God's system), you might fail or fall flat on your face.

Instead, when we abandon ourselves fully to God's kingdom, we find that the "operating system" He has created is eternal, redemptive, and always fruitful. It's not random, and it's not "hit or miss." There's a door that God opens, and we need to walk through it. It is a door that leads us out of the world's fallen, temporal system and into His eternal system (or kingdom). It doesn't mean that we will avoid suffering, mistakes, or hardship, but simply that we will operate in the God-inspired system of living that leads to the greatest spiritual and experiential outcomes.

Once I had this revelation, I made a conscious choice to operate in God's government and in His system. Since walking through that "kingdom door" (what Jesus calls the "narrow gateway" in Matthew 7:14), I have seen Him intervene in ways that defy human explanation. I have seen the "fuel" of the Holy Spirit take my family and me through hardships in ways we could not have ever imagined. I came through my challenging situation with an unshakeable confidence in the principles of His kingdom, His system. The result of my difficult business crisis was a journey I have now been traveling for more than twenty-five years. It has been an exciting and amazing journey of knowledge, wisdom, understanding, and relationship.

In fact, the first edition of this book was published just over a decade ago. Since then, God has revealed more insights to me that have led me to fully update and revise this volume. I have also updated and revised parts two and three of my other books in this series, *Kingdomnomics: The Dynamics of Conduct and Behavior,* and *Kingdom Deployment: Operating in Your Created Design for Your Eternal Purpose.* I encourage you to read those titles after this one, as they cover the full spectrum of what I call the Kingdom System.

This journey of learning about kingdom life was guided from the beginning by three pressing questions:

1. What is the kingdom of God and His system of government? (Addressed in this book)
2. What are the dynamics, principles, and disciplines that make the system effective in our lives? (Addressed in *Kingdomnomics*)
3. How do we display and present the kingdom in society? (Addressed in *Kingdom Deployment*)

The recorded written Word gives us the answers to these three questions, and His Spirit teaches us how to apply them. He has given us everything we need to deliver and employ the government of heaven on Earth. We do not have to lament that the kingdom is not here yet, let alone wonder when it will come. It came through Jesus, and we have access to it now.

From my research and experiences, I believe this is the piece of the puzzle that our heart longs for. It's what all of humanity is searching for whenever we think to ourselves, *I must be missing something; there has to be more to life than this.* I freely admit, however, that my research is not exhaustive and that there is much I still do not understand. The more I learn, the more I realize how much more there is to know. After all, we see through a glass darkly or "with a dim reflection," as it says in the Amplified Classic Edition (1 Corinthians 13:12).

Whatever insights you learn of God's kingdom on your journey, I am sure He will inspire you to share them with the rest of us. We are citizens of the great and magnificent government of the living God, and He rewards those who first seek His kingdom with its deepest and richest blessings.

One thing you will notice is that I do not refer to God's Word—His Holy Scriptures—as "the Bible." That is because I do no not believe that particular word captures the eternal, transformational power of God's Word. Nowhere in the Scriptures does the word "Bible" appear—which makes sense because they comprise dozens of writers who compiled their texts, scrolls, and letters over several thousand years. I also believe that throughout the centuries, mankind has heaped upon that word a lot of negative religious baggage. The word "Bible" can become a religious word like the Torah or Koran.

When I first wrote this book, I used the word "laws" quite often in reference to how God's kingdom operates on Earth and through the lives of Christians; however, since then, God has taken me through a radical "kingdom schooling," showing me that instead of the word "laws" to describe the structure and elements of His eternal kingdom, I needed to exchange it for the word "dynamics."

When the Holy Spirit God spoke this to me, I had no clue what He meant. He said to me, "Charlie, they *are* laws, but they are more dynamics than laws." The word "law" has a connotation that isn't accurate when you talk about Scripture. A law has to do with regulation and compliance, and that is not who God is.

After much study, here is my definition:

> **A dynamic is an interactive system involving competing and conflicting forces where your choice of action contains the inertia that takes you to a predetermined outcome.**

For example, gravity is a dynamic. You can pretend it does not exist, but the reality is that when dealing with gravity, you will always be engaging with a predetermined outcome: if you throw a stone in the air, it will come down. There's no debate, no argument, and no nuance. Whether you choose to honor the dynamic or not, the outcome is there. It's called the law of gravity, but it really is a dynamic.

What is the difference between laws and dynamics, you might ask? As it pertains to God's Kingdom System, the difference is the following:

- Laws are regulation-based, while dynamics are relationship-focused.
- Laws are restrictive, while dynamics are redemptive.
- Laws are about enforcing religion, while dynamics are about dispersing revelation.
- Laws are manmade, while dynamics are God-breathed.
- Laws are about income (transaction), while dynamics are about outcome (transformation).
- Laws can be altered and abolished, while dynamics have predetermined outcomes that are absolute.

- Laws are about compliance, while dynamics are about flourishment.

I am not saying that God does not give us laws. The Ten Commandments are commonly referred to as laws (or the Law). Therefore, I don't want to demonize the word "law" because laws have their purpose. (For example, it is a right and good law to make murder illegal.) We know that Jesus did not come to abolish the Law but to fulfill it. Laws are not bad; they are only an affront to the lawless; however, to those who are seeking God's kingdom above all else, they point us in the right direction.

For our purposes, God has made it clear to me that a major paradigm shift is needed for His Church to arise in these tumultuous times. For too long, the church has been mimicking the rules-based laws of the world, rather than the relationally based dynamics of God's kingdom. Though it might *seem* like semantics, I believe words matter a great deal. This is a scriptural concept, and the very first words of the New Testament say as much: "In the beginning the Word already existed. The Word was with God, and the Word was God" (John 1:1). The Word, of course, is Jesus.

There are only two systems in the world: the kingdom of God, and the kingdom of darkness. I basically missed this very important truth for the first fifty or so years of my life. As mentioned previously, I was a born-again Christian who unknowingly lived my life operating almost entirely by the rules of the "other kingdom" that is not God's Plan nor design. The output of this was confusion, frustration, blocked goals, and a life that was falling short of all He desired for me (i.e., my destiny).

I asked myself, how could I have been raised by loving Christian parents (which I was) yet still miss the essence of the Gospel (which I had)? Because over the two millennia since Christ came—and going back to the Garden—the enemy's goal has been to deceive and neutralize the people of God. The kingdom of this world is based on rules, laws, and religious practices of compliance. It is not eternal; it is not grace-giving; it is not the kingdom that Jesus brought to Earth. Without even knowing it, many Christians remain bound up, living their lives by the laws of the worldly kingdom.

Satan is defeated (which is why I will often refer to him as the defeated Satan), so his tools revolve around deception. But Jesus did not come to Earth to install religion, rule-following, and compliance. That is what Satan wants us to believe. It is his great lie. Rather, in God's system, *relationship* is the key—His grace and mercy have freed us from the bonds of the kingdom of darkness.

In the kingdom of God, the teaching of values, principles, and established precedents is more than information about laws involving regulation and rule-keeping. In our increasingly secularized society, the laws of man are shifting, self-defined, and relative. We believe that we can disobey them without consequence if no one sees us or if we do not get caught.

Dynamics are different. Dynamics operate by design. They are defined by cause and effect: they produce their results and their outcomes because of their design, and we cannot escape their predetermined outcomes. They are part of a system of competing or conflicting forces.

Our choice of conduct and behavior (the inertia) produces the predetermined outcome whether anyone is aware of our choice (inertia) or not. Even if no one sees us or will ever know of our actions, the outcome remains certain. For example, when we sin and ask God for forgiveness, the rules of the kingdom are fixed: that forgiveness is sealed in heaven. God doesn't need to think about it; He doesn't withhold forgiveness in exchange for something. When you make a choice in the kingdom, that choice contains within it the inertia that results in a predetermined outcome.

Knowing the facts (knowledge) and how to make that knowledge work personally for each of us is called wisdom for humanity. We are not helpless. We are not without hope. As we activate and appropriate God's eternal dynamics, we begin to operate in the correct choice to the alternative systems of the world.

Our Creator God is a God of systems. Everything that He has created and continues to create operates and functions within a system. Humanity has searched so desperately for something that will make a positive difference in the outcomes of their lives. For something that will allow them to have input and direct their outcomes. The Kingdom System is our Creator's plan and provision for this influence and is the only eternal answer to our challenges.

I mentioned earlier that I am a businessman and entrepreneur and that a business crisis is what led me to search for the "better Way" of God's kingdom. During this time of revelation, God also spoke to me about how I viewed my work. He said:

> **You are not called to pursue employment so you can earn an income.**
>
> **You are called to deployment so you can affect outcome—yours and others'.**

No matter how you earn a living and where you are in life, God wants to help you break free from the world's limited mindset and into a new paradigm of His eternal kingdom. In the process, I believe He will also show you that this life is indeed more than employment (doing work) and income (achieving "things"). It is about understanding and moving into the specific calling He has for you so you can be deployed for the greatest outcomes for you and for others.

Join with me as we explore the kingdom of God, how He designed it, how it operates in contrast to the world's failed system, and how you can walk in—and experience—His eternal kingdom with power, authority, and victory.

CHAPTER 1

WHAT IS THE KINGDOM?

During the reigns of those kings, the God of heaven will set up a kingdom that will never be destroyed or conquered. It will crush all these kingdoms into nothingness, and it will stand forever.

—Daniel 2:44 NLT

For the vast majority of man's existence, the night sky was pitch black and shone with stars. Try to imagine what Abraham saw when he left his tent and gazed into the night desert sky. With absolutely no light pollution the world over, it must have been a brilliant sight—particularly when the moon was waning or new. Today, even in the most remote corners of Earth—a hut deep in the Amazon or an outpost in Antarctica—satellites blink overhead.

In the United States, it wasn't until the late 1800s that homes were powered by electricity. It was used, at first, in parts of Manhattan among commercial properties and in the homes of the very wealthy; however, most families continued to light their homes with gas light and candles for fifty more years as the spread of the use of electricity was slow. By 1925, 42 years later, half of all homes in the U.S. were powered by electricity. Today, 87 percent of the world's households have access to electricity; in some nations, the number is far less. For example, only 52 percent of North Koreans have access, and in the war-torn nation of South Sudan, the number is only 7 percent.[9]

When Jesus came to Earth, his presence was the spiritual equivalent of the "electrical power" of Heaven being given to the world. Jesus brought with Him the eternal, redemptive, kingdom of God and "flipped on the lights" for all mankind to see, to understand, and to practice life in the kingdom. Prior to Jesus' arrival, the Light—Father God—was present, but His kingdom, His redemptive plan for governance had not yet come.

God provided signposts and prophetic pictures of His coming kingdom, and though God had not yet "turned on the electricity" that would illuminate the world, throughout the Old Testament He gave us prophetic glimpses of the coming eternal kingdom. They were like "lightning strikes" of His future Coming; pictures and flashes of the structure of God's kingdom to come.

At the time, the world was under the Mosaic Law of the Ten Commandments. We know, of course, that since the days of Adam, mankind had struggled to abide by God's laws. That's what created the need for Jesus' Coming and eventual sacrifice on the cross—once and for all. Jesus, the Lamb of God, paid the price for all of us through His death and resurrection.

Since Jesus' resurrection and ascension two millennia ago, the god of this age—the defeated Satan—has worked overtime to "dim the lights" on God's eternal and redemptive kingdom. A key tool has been religion—the layering on of rules and laws that counterfeit the true dynamics of God's kingdom. Using the analogy of electrical power, for 2,000 years the defeated Satan has attempted to "cut the power lines" so God's people are left in the darkness of tedious religion.

It's time to flip the lights back on so we can fully recognize, appropriate, and walk in the light of our eternal King. After all . . .

> *Every gift God freely gives us is good and perfect, streaming down from the Father of lights, who shines from the heavens with no hidden shadow or darkness and is never subject to change. God was delighted to give us birth by the truth of his infallible Word so that we would fulfill his chosen destiny for us and become the favorite ones out of all his creation!*
>
> —James 1:17–18, (TPT)

And what is the goal of the defeated Satan? To make us forget that we are, indeed, God's very own prized possession. Religion is simply the tool by which the enemy attempts to drive us toward rules rather than relationship; to darken our eyes to the fact that God has a powerful plan for each one of us. The more the defeated Satan can distract us from the true light of God's love, and fill us with burdensome religion, the less we are able to possess God's kingdom destiny for us.

Kingdoms Old, Kingdom Eternal

Some six hundred years before the birth of Jesus, the Book of Daniel provided a powerful prophetic "lightning strike" that illuminated the reality of God's kingdom. In fact, God used the prophet Daniel to reveal one of the most vivid pictures of the kingdom of God. The story itself is remarkable as its protagonist is enslaved in mighty Babylon, then elevated by God to a position of influence and power. In fact, Daniel was a captive Israelite plucked from among the conquered men of Judah, who was then trained to serve the king himself.

Daniel's overseer was Ashpenaz, the chief eunuch of the court, who gave Daniel the Babylonian name Belteshazzar—which translates to "Lady, protect the king." He purposefully gave Daniel a woman's name to mock the foreign slave with the mysterious religion. Despite this, God gave Daniel something far better: an understanding of His eternal kingdom.

Daniel heard the news that was racing through the streets of Babylon: King Nebuchadnezzar had a dream and was searching for someone to interpret it. The king had become increasingly impatient and angry as his astrologers and soothsayers were too afraid to offer a guess. One of his more clever wise men said, "Let the king tell his servants the dream, and we will give its interpretation." But this only made Nebuchadnezzar more furious as he insisted that someone be found who could both describe the dream and provide its meaning. If they failed, they would be cut to pieces and their horses slaughtered and made into ash.

Because everyone had refused to offer an interpretation, the king issued a decree that all the wise men of Babylon were to be put to death. Daniel, an outsider and a captive from Judah who worshipped a single God called YHWH, stepped up. He approached Arioch, the captain of the king's guard, and asked for a bit of time to bring the king the answers he sought.

That evening, Daniel called upon "the revealer of mysteries" for help, and God told him the dream and the interpretation. The dream was about four coming kingdoms, governments, that would be coming upon Earth. Nebuchadnezzar was so impressed that he prostrated himself before Daniel, saying, "Truly your God *is* the God of gods, the

Lord of kings, and a revealer of secrets, since you could reveal this secret" (Daniel 2:47). Because of Daniel's prophetic accuracy, he was promoted by the king and became ruler (magistrate or governor) of the province of Babylon and chief administrator over all the wise men of Babylon.

When we examine Daniel's interpretation of the dream a bit deeper, we discover that it was a startling, accurate prediction that the Medes and Persians would come after the current Babylonian Empire, then the Greeks, and later the Romans. Four earthly kingdoms with distinct governments.

In the age of the Roman Empire, God would set up a kingdom on the earth that would never be destroyed or occupied. It would be an everlasting, eternal kingdom that would never end. It would break all other kingdoms into pieces and stand forever. God's kingdom would grow larger than all the others and last for eternity.

It is not difficult for us to understand that the first four kingdoms represented in Nebuchadnezzar's dream were governments. They were not mysterious, invisible realms but real, functioning kingdoms on the earth. It only makes sense that the greatest kingdom that was still to come and surpass them all would also be a government. It is God's government, the government of heaven. It does not function exactly as others do, but it is nevertheless a government.

What I did not learn while growing up in church was that God's kingdom has very practical implications here on Earth. Daniel prophesied that this "eternal kingdom" would come during the era of the Roman Empire, and that it would smash all other kingdoms.

That kingdom, of course, came through the Person of Jesus Christ.

> *For to us a Child is born, to us a Son is given; and the government shall be upon His shoulder, and His name shall*

be called Wonderful Counselor, Mighty God, Everlasting Father [of Eternity], Prince of Peace.

--Isaiah 9:6, AMPC

An Understanding of the Kingdom

As I shared in the introduction, the Holy Spirit God led me on a search through the written Word to learn about His kingdom, His system. While in the midst of a difficult situation—a hostile business group was trying to sabotage our work and ruin much of what we had worked for—I began to ask Holy Spirit questions: "What am I missing? What am I not seeing? What do I not know that I need to know? Where should I look?"

I searched the Scriptures, looking for every mention of His system (especially in Jesus' teachings about the kingdom) throughout the gospels. I had always understood that when Jesus comes again (i.e., His Second Coming), He will, then, establish His rule and reign—not before. Once I overcame years of assumptions and incorrect teachings by sincere-hearted people to read with a fresh perspective, however, I learned that is inaccurate.

What I discovered was that there are prophetic signs and brilliant flashes of Jesus and His kingdom throughout both the Old Testament—as seen in Daniel 2—and the New Testament. These prophetic signposts point to an indestructible kingdom that would arise during the rule of the Roman Empire.

The first reference in the New Testament to this "indestructible kingdom" is uttered by John the Baptist, the precursor to Jesus, when he proclaimed that "the kingdom of God is at hand" (Matthew 3:2). While the Jews were looking for a messiah (lowercase "m") who would help them throw off the yoke of Roman rule, John was preaching an entirely different gospel—one centered on a coming spiritual, yet tangible and effective kingdom, and based on a correct understanding of the Scriptures.

This was just before Jesus asked John to baptize Him, and when the Holy Spirit descended upon Jesus "like a dove" (Matthew 3:17), thus signifying the beginning of Jesus' ministry. As I continued my search through the Word, I realized that the kingdom came with Jesus. It was not a future event, but a kingdom that was established two millennia ago. In other words, the kingdom of God is here, now.

Isaiah 9:6 tells us that when Jesus came, He brought God's government "upon His shoulders." It came with Him. The next verse tells us that His government will never stop increasing. This is not a prediction of something that *might* happen; it is a certainty. "The zeal of the Lord of hosts will perform this" (Isaiah 9:7, AMPC). Here's the critical point:

> God is zealous about bringing His government to Earth.

As I read these things, I began to realize that the timing of the kingdom of God is not "one day in heaven;" it is available now. It is something that has already happened—or has, at least, begun to happen. It is available now. We can live under His government—that is, in His system—even while we live on Earth during this age.

I also began to realize that the kingdom of God is the government of heaven. It is God's actual government, His rule, and His reign. Jesus brought this kingdom to Earth. This realization that God's kingdom has already begun was a huge turning point in both my life and in Fran's as well.

Jesus told us to pray for God's kingdom to come and for God's will to be done "on earth as it is in heaven" (Matthew 6:10). In doing so, He was telling us to call upon all the power and the forces of the government of heaven and to pray that the government of God would intervene in our situations, our circumstances, and our relationships. Jesus was telling us that His will would be accomplished here and now, just as it is in heaven.

Kingdoms Are Governments

Here is one of the definitions Merriam Webster uses for government:

> *the organization, machinery, or agency through which a political unit exercises authority and performs functions and which is usually classified according to the distribution of power within it.*[10]

I like this definition because it emphasizes that a government is organized and exercises authority according to a power structure. In the kingdom of God, there is but one power source and Ruler who is benevolent in His governance. In God's eternal kingdom, His reign and rule are clear, organized, just, and authoritative. And though His kingdom is by no means a democracy, He chooses to partner with us, the citizens of the kingdom, to do His good works.

In relation to government, I want to look at this term "the kingdom of God"—or "the kingdom of heaven"—more closely. What establishes something as a kingdom? In the Scriptures, the term is almost always applied to a government. Daniel's interpretation of Nebuchadnezzar's dream was about four successive human governments after which the God of heaven would establish His own government.

Nebuchadnezzar ruled over the Babylonian Empire, which was

followed by the rule of the Medes and Persian Empire, then the Greek Empire under the Macedonian Alexander the Great. The rule of the Roman Empire followed the Greek and was the dominant government at the time of Christ. All of these empires were human governments that controlled a certain territory. It is correct to say that the use of "kingdom" in this passage is a rule of law, culture, and influence that functions as a government.

Most of us in modern Western society have never experienced a kingdom as a form of government. When we hear the word "kingdom," we envision castles and moats and medieval knights riding white horses and carrying huge swords. To us, this is an outdated system that has little place in our democratic world. God, however, is not the president or prime minister of a democracy. He is the King. The only kind of government that is suitable and will work for a king is a kingdom.

The Scriptures, God's Word, are not religious but are relational. They describe two distinct and wholly separate kingdoms, one legitimate King, and one who wants to be king. From beginning to end, the dominant and constant theme in the Scriptures is the epic battle for kingship over humanity by this rebel and wannabe king. So ultimately, the Word of God is not really a book about religion; it is a book about government. Who will rule this rebellious people? Which king will you serve? Which kingdom will prevail in your life? What are the dynamics, rights, and privileges of the kingdom we were meant to live in? From beginning to end, the story of Scripture is the story of kingdom conflict.

The phrase "kingdom of God" or "kingdom of heaven" is not found in the Old Testament, but it appears more than 100 times in the four gospels. Jesus taught about the kingdom more than any other theme and told many parables with the kingdom as their theme. Jesus' first words in the gospel of Mark are, "The time is fulfilled, and the kingdom of

God is at hand" (Mark 1:15). As mentioned previously, John the Baptist heralded the kingdom coming. In this verse, we see Jesus confirming that the kingdom is already here. The coming kingdom was the focus of Jesus' preaching, teaching, and ministry.

Jesus was not talking about a specific area of land, of course. We cannot equate the kingdom of God with the Holy Land or Israel or the church. Jesus was talking about a system of government—God's rule and reign by the "agency or power structure" of heaven on Earth through the engagement of faith by His kingdom citizens—and He emphasized through His teaching that He was bringing the kingdom with Him. In fact, He indicated several times that it was already among us.

It seems very clear that Jesus came into the world not to establish a religion but to establish a kingdom—a government. He was bringing His kingdom—the kingdom that already exists and reigns in heaven—to reestablish His rule on Earth. Though God had many purposes in coming to Earth as Jesus, every act of the Messiah would lead to the establishment of God's government here in this earthly realm.

We cannot be content to say that heaven is the realm of God's government and Earth is the realm of Satan and his demons, although many seem to believe that. That is an incomplete understanding of redemption and restoration. Jesus said the kingdom of God is here, now. He told us to pray that God's kingdom would come on Earth, just as it is in heaven. God's kingdom is wherever He rules and reigns, and He intends to rule and reign everywhere.

If God's kingdom is a government that is meant to be implemented on Earth, then we need to understand the nature of government. This raises critical questions:

1. What does a government do?

2. What does it provide?
3. How does it enforce its laws or dynamics?
4. How does this government impact our daily lives?
5. What kind of government is this, and what characteristics does it have?
6. If God's government is ruling on Earth, why do we experience so many of the effects from the kingdom of darkness?

We will spend the rest of this book exploring these questions, but for now we need to understand that we can already live under God's government. The false kingdom of the enemy has not gone away, but the kingdom of God has broken in upon it and has authority over it! Living under the government of heaven is a legitimate option for us. Right now.

Which System?

Are you struggling with pain, loss, or sin patterns in your life? Whatever it is, if it does not exist in heaven, then it is not part of God's eternal plan. Heaven has no sickness, strife, addiction, broken relationships, lack of resources, or suffering; these are not God's ultimate purposes for our lives.

Jesus clearly intended for us to be able to live in the kingdom of heaven now, not just one day after we die. That does not mean we will not encounter obstacles or experience challenges in this world, but those hurdles are not meant to overcome us. They are opportunities for us to bring the government of heaven into our experience now.

Most people do not realize they have the option of living in a different system from the one they are currently living in, but they do. I did not realize that I had the option, or the ability, to choose to live in God's kingdom, now, when I was walking through the season of futility in my business. What I was experiencing did not line up with what Jesus said about me in His Word. His Word says I am more than a conqueror (Romans 8:37) and that my faith overcomes the world (1 John 5:4), but it did not look like I was conquering or overcoming anything.

I believed His truth, but I did not know how to apply it to the circumstances in my life. For example, imagine wanting to flyfish but only ever reading about it in books or online. Never picking up a pole, never dipping a line, never catching a fish. Can one say they have flyfished if they have never even held a pole?

Like nearly everyone else, though I knew deep in my spirit that I was missing some piece of the puzzle, I thought that was how life was meant to be. When God began teaching me about His government, I realized I had another option. He told me that I was part of His system of redemptive kingdom government, but I was operating under the rules and laws of the enemy's kingdom. I was giving the false king license to kill, steal, and destroy. I had to choose to begin living under the dynamics of God's government.

A good father does not give his children responsibilities without also giving them a way to fulfill them. A good king does not give his citizens a task or assignment without giving them the means to complete it. Somehow, most of us who acknowledge God as our Father and King are living with an apparent inability to do the things He has called us to do and to experience the promises He has given to us. Our experience may not line up with the description He gave us of our position and relationship with Him.

I can tell you from firsthand experience, when what you believe does not align with the way you live, misery can prevail. Proverbs says that hope deferred makes the heart sick, but when the desire comes, it is a tree of life (Proverbs 13:12). Without hope, the heart grows weary and tired. I believe this in my core: if you are not seeing the reality of God's promises manifesting in your life, an adjustment is needed.

I am not trying to bash on you. Just the opposite. My entire impetus for writing is to say, "Friend, you do not need to go through life as a functional 'kingdom agnostic' like I was, without the reality of God's kingdom activated and empowered in your life." Also, there are not "ten steps you need to follow" to inculcate the reality of the kingdom in your life. More than constructing an elaborate system, it is like turning on a light. As you delve into the reality of what Jesus says about the kingdom, the light of its truth will illuminate your heart. And we serve a loving God, within whom there is no shifting shadow.

Why do many Christians live as if the kingdom is a future event? If you do not think that is true, imagine putting fifty born-again believers and fifty people claiming no faith, agnostics, in a room together, then giving all one hundred people a questionnaire about their lives and the things that are important to them—their finances, health, relationships, interests, careers, sense of fulfillment, and so on. If you read the questionnaires, would you be able to tell the believers from the other half? Probably not.

As believers, we have come up with many explanations for why we cannot direct and impact the outcomes in our lives. If we are honest, the metrics of a typical Christian's relationships, health, and financial situation look much like the metrics for non-believers. One statistic that serves as a veritable warning of potential crisis of faith is marriage. The divorce rate among Christians has been slowly increasing on those who are not Christian.

Faith comes by hearing the Word of God, not by what someone says about religion. And "hearing" means more than listening; it means to absorb, believe, and act upon the promises in God's Word. When we are unengaged with the Father (e.g., not reading the Scriptures, not praying, not spending time with Him, not interacting with fellow believers), it will affect the type and amount of spiritual fruit in our lives.

When God came to the earth as Jesus Christ - Emmanuel - He delivered to humanity the ability to fulfill His initial mandate given to them at Creation. Do you remember what that was? We were to live on the earth in power, authority, and dominion. We were to fill the earth and subdue it. We were to have dominion over every living thing except other humans. We were to be His partners in governing this planet. (See Genesis 2, AMPC.)

He still gives us that option. To take it, we must choose to live by His system.

Our Mission: His Kingdom Come

We may call ourselves believers, but we are much more than that. We are citizens of God's kingdom. A king, whether good or bad, is judged by how well he takes care of his citizens and how He provides for them. Jesus is our King. He has provided for all our needs—spiritually, relationally, emotionally, financially, physically. Everything. All our needs come through this kingdom relationship.

Many of us, however, may be experiencing the fruit of another kingdom. Satan is the father of lies, and the only power he has is through deception. If he can get people to believe his lies, then he has license to steal, kill, and destroy. Satan can keep us enslaved to things that fit his own kingdom, and as a result, inhibit our ability to connect to God's kingdom system of government.

So, I will ask again: What are you struggling with? Is it family dysfunction? Financial stress? Health issues? Whatever your challenge is, if it does not exist in heaven, it should not exist in your life. The key to activating your life into a kingdom relationship is to learn how to call heaven to Earth and how to live under God's governmental system according to His kingdom directions and His designed dynamics. When we do this, the manifestation of any other kingdom will not exist in our lives.

One of the reasons few people recognize the truth of the dynamic of kingdom relationship is that for centuries, the church has done a good job of teaching the gospel of redemption but not a very good job of teaching the gospel of restoration. We have taught the truth that the blood of Christ paid for our sins and purchased our salvation … that redemption cleanses us from sin and makes us capable of full fellowship with our Creator God. This is a wonderful truth. The only way to enter God's kingdom is to believe this truth and receive His grace through faith. When we do, we are born again (See John 3:16.); our spirit is made new, and the once-broken fellowship with God is now restored.

But redemption is not the entirety of the gospel message. Jesus also came to restore us. The written Word teaches both redemption *and* restoration. When Jesus was put into the tomb, He descended into hell and took the keys of the kingdom. That was Satan's ultimate defeat. From that day forward, the defeated Satan cannot ever be considered victorious in anything; he is a defeated foe. Satan's identity is as a defeated deceiver. In contrast, Ephesians 1:1 calls Christians "saints"; we are, right now, seated with Christ in the heavenlies (Ephesians 2:6). We are hidden with Christ in God (Colossians 3:3). That is my identity and yours: do not let Satan convince you that you deserve his identity. You do not!

Jesus told His followers that He had the keys of the kingdom, then He sent them into the world with the message of His kingdom. That message includes the gospel of salvation as we have long understood it and so much more. "Salvation" in Scripture is a holistic word that can include every area of life. Jesus' resurrection is a powerful picture of restoration—a body alive from the dead. The empty tomb is proof of our restoration. We are restored to our relationship as it was before sin and evil entered the world, and we are reunited with God Himself. We have original glory instead of original sin.

I want to emphasize that this does not mean we will never suffer. The apostles suffered, great Christians throughout history have suffered, and so will we because we live in a fallen world. However, we do not have to be defeated by suffering. At times, Satan will manifest adverse situations and conditions that look real, feel real, and have real effects in our lives. But he is not presenting the truth. Those manifestations are illegitimate because they come from a defeated enemy.

To overcome the schemes of the enemy, we must learn to see beyond what our Earth-born eyes can see. We will notice all kinds of obstacles and contradictions in the earthly realm, but we should never put our focus on them. Our focus must be on the King who overcame the enemy and this world. When we choose to look at Him and believe what He says about us and what He has promised us, we are choosing to live under His government. Kingdom kind of faith overcomes the lies of the enemy, and sooner or later his manifestations must disappear. Consider this powerful verse from James: "So humble yourselves before God. Resist the devil, and he will flee from you." (James 4:7). Notice the two steps to getting Satan to flee:

1. **Humble yourself before God.** Submission carries negative connotations in our culture, but in God's kingdom, it simply means to acknowledge His rule and reign and defer to it.

2. **Resist the devil.** Even if you have been struggling with a secret sin or addiction, the devil does not "own" you nor have absolute power over you. If you kill rats in an alleyway but do not get rid of the garbage, what happens? The rats come back. The same thing is true of resisting the devil. We must get rid of the garbage so the rats—or, in this case, Satan and his agents—have no reason to return.

Though outside the scope of the subject of this book, I encourage you to research passages related to your identity in Christ. It is an inside-out job. As the Holy Spirit renews your mind, you will live increasingly in the reality of God's kingdom, and you will have more victory over the sins of this world. The more you understand that you are resurrected and that your identity has been restored, the more you will be able to reject the false kingdom of the deceiver.

> *We view our slight, short-lived troubles in the light of eternity. We see our difficulties as the substance that produces for us an eternal, weighty glory far beyond all comparison, because we don't focus our attention on what is seen but on what is unseen. For what is seen is temporary, but the unseen realm is eternal.*
>
> —2 Corinthians 4:17-18 (TPT)

The written Word instructs us to believe and to confess what we believe. I love the following two verses about activating your belief:

The heart that believes in him receives the gift of the righteousness of God—and then the mouth confesses, resulting in salvation.

—Romans 10:10 (TPT)

They conquered him completely through the blood of the Lamb and the powerful word of his testimony. They triumphed because they did not love and cling to their own lives, even when faced with death.

—Revelation 12:11 (TPT)

We overcome those adverse situations and conditions that have real effects in our lives by faith and by confessing what we know to be true.

God gave us the authority to enlist all of heaven into our lives on Earth. Heaven's resources—angel armies, spiritual power, the Word of God, and the Spirit within us—are at our disposal for every situation, each circumstance, and each of our relationships. When we encounter a challenge to our well-being, we normally attack it with our mind, our thoughts, our emotions, and our intellect; however, we are not supposed to relate to God primarily with our mind, but also with our spirit. John 4 says we must worship Him in—or out of—our spirit and in His Word. That is what our relationship with Him is based upon. When we face the enemy's lies and manifestations, we must exercise the spiritual authority we have been given in Christ.

Notice, when Paul instructs us on how to battle the enemy, he often refers to the mind:

For although we live in the natural realm, we don't wage a military campaign employing human weapons, using

> *manipulation to achieve our aims. Instead, our spiritual weapons are energized with divine power to effectively dismantle the defenses behind which people hide. We can demolish every deceptive* fantasy *that opposes God and break through every arrogant* attitude *that is raised up in defiance of the true* knowledge *of God. We capture, like prisoners of war, every* thought *and insist that it bow in obedience to the Anointed One. Since we are armed with such dynamic weaponry, we stand ready to punish any trace of rebellion, as soon as you choose complete obedience.*
>
> —2 Corinthians 10:3–6 (TPT; emphases mine)

The words I have emphasized all have to do with the mind. This is where Satan attacks, and therefore, we must battle the enemy here through the power of the Holy Spirit God. We do this when we submit to His kingdom rule and authority, then through the power vested in us as a citizen of His kingdom. Resist the devil and his schemes, and walk in the liberty provided in His kingdom.

Our Connection to the King

Most people believe their purpose is to live so they can get to heaven. That is not what Jesus taught. He said to honor God who is in heaven and pray for His kingdom—His rule, His authority, His sovereignty, and His redemptive, Kingdom System of government—to come to the earth so that things on Earth would be as they are in heaven. This is the essence of the Lord's Prayer that He gave us in Matthew 6. We can apply heaven's jurisdiction to earthly situations.

This is a very relational approach. In talking about living under a "system" of government with all its dynamics and laws, there is a danger in giving the impression that the faith life is a matter of simply following the right principles. Please understand the context of this government. It is more than living in a kingdom; it is a living relationship with the living King. We do not stand outside the castle walls and hope to catch a glimpse of the king standing in a distant tower. Our King invites us in. We have access to Him 24/7, and He longs to spend time with us.

When we become a citizen of God's kingdom, we are filled with the Holy Spirit God. He then releases His power within us, allowing us to accomplish His desires. He then directs us in our desires. It is our connection with Him, through relationship and fellowship, that gives us access to the keys of the kingdom. This is really about a Person, not a process. It is about the Person of Jesus—a man whom we can relate to through the Kingdom System that He has provided for us.

I am blessed to have been married to Fran, my beautiful bride, for more than fifty years. We made the choice early in our relationship to be together in everything. We do almost everything together, and we like it that way. We choose activities and relationships that allow us to honor that choice. We know what each other is thinking without speaking. A look, a glance, a general communication between our spirits happens naturally and without effort. This has been our experience for most of the five decades we have been together.

Imagine what would have happened if I had taken Fran home from our wedding ceremony and said, "Now Fran, here you are. This nice home is yours. You stay here. Do not leave. Do not come out where people can see you. I will meet with you only here, except in emergency situations. On Sundays, I will come here to see you. I cannot promise every Sunday, just some Sundays. While here, I will not speak with you. I will listen to someone else speak about you. During the week, maybe Wednesdays, I will come by if it is convenient for me. I will stop by occasionally. But again, as on the Sunday visits, I will not speak to you. I will listen to someone else speak about you.

"But, Fran, we must be clear how this relationship works. If I need you to perform, I expect you to be ready immediately without question or delay. I want a large family. If I need you to cook and to entertain many guests, to take care of me, the babies, or our parents when they are sick, or whatever else I need, you must be ready and willing."

If you were to overhear this, you would probably say, "What a one-sided, unreasonable request! Fran is not his slave. She is not there just for his convenience. Where is the love? Where is the relationship in that arrangement?" I am confident Fran would not accept such an arrangement either.

If we do not expect this of the person we marry, why do we expect it of the God who created us, loves us more than we can imagine, and wants to spend time with us?

God Is the God of Relationship

- Relationship requires fellowship.
- Fellowship requires time spent together.
- Time spent together requires we give the time.
- Time is given to us; time is ours to give as we decide.

That is how we must relate to God or anyone else we want to know intimately. Many people try to maintain a relationship with God by visiting Him and talking to Him, occasionally, then expecting Him to answer whenever they need Him. I call this the "spare tire" agreement. We take it out in an emergency or when we need it. No wonder they have a hard time hearing His voice! Getting to know the Lord, or anyone else, requires significant time and fellowship. That is how we develop a relationship with the King and learn about His ways.

Living under this heavenly government is, first and foremost, a matter of relating to God. It is also a matter of understanding how His kingdom works. There are dynamics of the kingdom that apply to everyone, just as there are universal dynamics of physics. You can choose to obey or disobey the universal dynamics of the earth, but the consequences are not optional. Everyone who jumps off a building will experience, firsthand, the dynamic of gravity.

Likewise, we experience consequences when we keep or violate the dynamics of the kingdom like unforgiveness and giving. With most physical and mathematical dynamics, we experience the results and outcomes immediately, but that is not always the case with the dynamics of the kingdom. The effects may not be revealed until years later. Still, eventually we arrive at a predictable outcome. This is what God began to teach me during a stressful season in my life when very little made sense.

I am still learning what it means to live in His kingdom. I have seen His heavenly government manifested on Earth, and I know these truths work. It is possible for us to live beyond Earth's realm and experience the miraculous of heaven's realm in our everyday lives. It should be normal for us to overcome the deceptions and manifestations of the ungodly kingdom that illegitimately remains on this planet.

When we focus, by faith, on what God has said, we begin to experience the things He has promised us. Faith is the substance of things hoped for and the evidence of things not seen (Hebrews 11:1). When we learn to live by faith, the unseen kingdom of God and heaven's realm becomes visible in our lives. His will is done on Earth just as it is in heaven.

Kingdom Activating Declarations

Toward the end of some chapters, we will offer truths that God wants to fully implant in our hearts and minds. As an exercise of faith, we will declare these truths out loud so they can manifest in our lives. This is not a "name and claim it" tactic. Because it has power, we speak the Word of our God. Because the demonic realm cannot read our minds, when we speak His Word, it serves notice to the enemy that he has no place in our lives. Most of these declared truths will involve our identity, our position, how we think, and how we choose to live out our life of faith. Let's begin with some foundational statements about the kingdom that help us understand God's kingdom purposes:

Whether you are gathered with others or reading alone, declare these truths of Kingdom System understanding out loud:

YOUR DECLARATIONS

KINGDOM SYSTEM UNDERSTANDING

God created the heavens and the earth and everything in them. He created man and woman, gave them dominion and authority, and instructed them to rule over Earth and everything on it. Everything on Earth belonged to God because He created it all; and because He owned everything, He could do with it as He wished. He chose to give humanity authority and dominion over all the earth. (Genesis 1:1, 26-28; John 1:2-3; Psalm 115:16)

Man gave the dominion and authority that God had given him to rule over Earth to Satan (Genesis 3:6). It was disobedience that separated human beings from God. What man lost through disobedience was his relationship with God. Because all dominion and authority are relational, humanity lost both. God is the God of relationship; He created and designed man for that purpose. Relationship requires fellowship; fellowship requires time spent together, and time spent together requires the commitment to give the time. There are no shortcuts. No relationship equals no authority nor dominion.

God Himself came to Earth in the person of Jesus Christ, Emmanuel, God with Us. Jesus engaged and defeated Satan and took back the dominion and authority man had given to him. Having defeated Satan, God gave access to that authority and dominion back to man. (Matthew 16:19; Luke 10:19)

While the man/God was on Earth in the person of Jesus, He established and delivered the system whereby human beings can live on the earth in complete victory and in a living relationship with our living God. That system is the redemptive kingdom governmental system of our God. (Matthew 12:27-28; Luke 16:1-15)

All governments have laws and commands that must be obeyed to be in the correct, or right, relationship with the ruling government and to receive the benefits offered by that government. These laws (dynamics) and commands are clearly shown and easy to understand. They are written in the book of our "Constitution" given to humanity by our God and our King. We know this book as the Scriptures.

All of the declarations found here, and many more, are available in the book Kingdom Activating Declarations by Charlie Lewis.

Visit www.ksam.net for this and other great resources.

CHAPTER 2

CHARACTERISTICS OF THE KINGDOM

But seek (aim at and strive after) first of all His kingdom and His righteousness (His way of doing and being right), and then all these things taken together will be given you besides.

—Matthew 6:33 (AMPC)

I was beginning my first year at university, and I had the next few years of my life all mapped out. I had spent an entire day planning for as much of the future as a seventeen-year-old can foresee. I went back to my car, laid my plans down on the seat, and said to myself, "Got it."

I was not even thinking about God, but I heard His voice. He spoke clearly to me:

"Where do I fit in here?"

I was so startled that I sat still for a long time, thinking, *I do not know, Lord. Do You want to fit in there?*

I did not know how to respond. I had not even considered what God "fitting in" my life might look like. I had been raised religiously, had attended church most of my life, and I knew about God. I had what I believed was a relationship with Him. But eventually, I discovered that I was not in a relationship. I was in a religion. At that time, Fran and I were dating, and we both knew we wanted to serve God. Beyond that, I certainly had not invited Him into my life plans.

I did not think I would have to go to Viet Nam. Yes, a war was going on, and a lot of my friends were getting drafted, but there was a system in place to determine who would go. Basically, you had to be "in phase" to avoid the draft, which meant you needed a certain quantity of successful college hours, or course credits, inside a certain period of time.

By this time, I had been in college for a year and a half, and I was definitely past being in phase. But because I changed colleges and went back to work in another town, the mail did not keep up with me. By the time I received my draft notice, it was time for me to report for a physical. It was a shock, to say the least.

This kind of mix-up was not uncommon, and when I explained my situation at the military base where my physical was being conducted, I was told that I could certainly appeal the draft selection decision. I was also informed that I would probably be finished with basic training by the time the appeal was even considered. I could have fought it—with the right connections, I am sure I could have won my appeal. But I was young, and I decided it was not worth it. I believed in the concept of serving my country, so I did not resist or protest.

Even more importantly, as I prayed about my situation, I believed that I should honor my draft status and serve my country. Was it my plan? Absolutely not. Still, God honored my decision as I became an officer and served as the airfield commander of a stage field near the Cambodian border. I was barely twenty but had several pilots working for me.

My intention is not to boast. Just the opposite. If left up to me, I would not have even been in Viet Nam. But that is where God placed me, and I believe there is a lot to be said for following His plan rather than my own. Oftentimes in His kingdom, we only see a glimpse of His plan at any given moment. But when we look back, we see it much more clearly. In my case, God threw me into the deep end—going to war in a foreign country—to increase my faith and prepare me for what was to come. Now, some fifty years after I left the hostile environment of Southeast Asia, I see the symmetry and purpose of God's plan.

Fran and I were married on July 4, 1969. For many people our age, it was the height of the hippie movement—Flower Power, Woodstock, and free love. For Fran and me, though, it was a very different experience. Fran had just graduated high school, and I was just a few years older than her. We loved each other very much, and we loved God but had little understanding of His kingdom or how it operated.

I had already been through officer's training, and immediately after we were married, I entered flight school. Just over a year later, I shipped out to Viet Nam. Before I left, Fran suffered a miscarriage of twin babies. The day she was released from the hospital, I picked her up, and we drove to the mall to have our picture taken. Fran says that day her pale skin against her white dress made her look like a ghost, but to me, she looked like an angel.

From there, we drove to the airport and said our goodbyes. We did not know if we would ever see each other again. That is not meant to sound dramatic—it was the simple reality of our situation. Thankfully,

I served my time in Viet Nam without physical injury, and upon my return, God began to take Fran and me down what Jesus calls the narrow path (or gate):

> *You can enter God's Kingdom only through the narrow gate. … But the gateway to life is very narrow and the road is difficult, and only a few ever find it.*
>
> —Matthew 7:13-14 (TPT)

The narrow gate is His pathway—through obedience, prayer, determination, and hard work, we made our way. Thankfully, despite our young ages, we both committed to stay on that narrow road—even when it hurt and pain pressed us hard, and even when it did not make sense. We learned that like with Abraham and countless others in the Scriptures, God rarely shows us the entire path. We see the next bend in the road, the next dip, the next curve but little beyond.

God led us to leave the comfort and status of a military officer's life and to trade it for a new civilian life working alongside my family in the furniture businesses in Florida. But that was our beginning, and we made the most of it. Little did we know that despite our lack of understanding of so many things about His kingdom, He would be faithful. We were embarking upon an amazing adventure that would open our eyes to the reality of something utterly transformative: the power and glory of His redemptive, eternal kingdom.

As I look back now, I realize that the encounter with God in my car was Him calling me to begin my journey into intimacy with Him. Almost unconsciously, it was the start of my pursuit of not only His plan for my life but my place in His kingdom. I now know that God wanted to show me how to change my thinking. He wanted to teach me about seeking His kingdom first, above all else. It would take years to really understand what that meant, and the understanding continues daily, but He at least showed me that He wanted to be the priority in my life. I sought the kingdom as knowingly as I could by learning to follow His voice.

I believe many people—most people would, in fact, be an accurate statement—are in the uncertain position of wanting to pursue the kingdom of God and an intimate, living relationship with our God but not knowing exactly what that is and what that looks like. Matthew 6:33 tells us to seek His kingdom first, before all else. Jesus delivers this message during the Sermon on the Mount, the context being with regards to one's earthly needs and worries. Jesus sets up a clear distinction between living as part of an earthly kingdom—in this sense, under the occupation of Rome—and God's redemptive eternal kingdom.

Jesus is urging us to make our relationship with God our highest priority. To do that well, it helps to know what the kingdom is. We need to know the story behind the kingdom conflict in this world, and we need to understand God's agenda for bringing His kingdom to Earth. Here, He conveyed a critical dynamic, or principle, through His words and actions. It can be summed up in this comparison:

Satan's kingdom is asset-based and time-driven.
God's kingdom is purpose-based and eternity-driven.

The purpose-based and eternity-driven approach produces far greater assets than pursuing assets alone will ever provide. Like everything that has to do with the defeated Satan, his ways are always destructive and deceptive. But when we align ourselves with Jesus as our Good Shepherd, and attune our ear to hear His voice, we discover that His Way is the true path toward doing and being right.

God's Government History

When was the last time you read the first few chapters of Genesis? Right from the beginning of His Word, God's relationship with humankind is one of covenant—a relationship that goes beyond casual commitment. Indeed, covenant means lifelong—forever. It is a commitment that says, "I love you; I want the best for you; and I want to be in relationship with you."

In the beginning, God created human beings and gave us dominion over the earth. Because He created the earth and everything in it, He had ownership and rulership of everything. It was not, nor has God's government ever been, a democracy. No vote is taken; God has provided the directions and instructions. Authority over Earth was His to give, and He gave it to the first humans. That is covenant. In other words, God did not have to give us authority here, but He chose to. He did not give us ultimate authority. He has not left His throne, and He remains sovereign over everything in His creation.

Just as a king gives other high-ranking people in his kingdom the authority to represent him, to make decisions, and to implement His policies, God gave Adam and Eve responsibility to implement God's rule over the territory of Earth. A covenant relationship was forged—it was humanity who acted outside of the covenant, not God. Over and over in the Old Testament, we see this theme of covenant and its role in God's desire to restore intimate relationship with His people. We know, of course, that despite giving us multiple chances to restore and keep covenant with God, we did not. Thus, the ultimate sacrificial Lamb was sent.

Not only does God have the right of ownership over the earth and all that is in it, but He also has the responsibility to provide for all the needs of His creation. A king is judged by the quality and abundance of his provision for the citizens of his kingdom. Our God is the perfect example of the perfect King, both in provision and supply. Nothing is lacking in Him—neither spiritually, mentally, emotionally, physically, financially, relationally, nor any other way. We do not need to look to anyone or anything else for our provision.

Humanity did not honor this authority and succumbed to Satan's temptation in the Garden of Eden, in effect giving him the keys of authority of the kingdom that we were supposed to hold. We broke covenant, and it had disastrous consequences. All dominion is relational, and the act of disobedience in the garden damaged the covenantal relationship between God and humanity. Adam and Eve did not lose their religion; they lost something more precious—their relationship with God. Before the fall, nothing separated humanity from being in perfect relationship with the King. Adam and Eve fellowshipped with Him in the cool of the evening, strolling through the beautiful garden God had prepared for them.

Western culture has developed a high disregard for authority, and today many people treat laws and instructions casually; however, God responded strongly to Adam and Eve's disobedience. His government was based on His transferring His authority and His instructions, and humanity's defiance against those instructions was a tragic mistake.

It is often said that it is easier to ask forgiveness than permission. Many people today give little thought to "minor" offenses like fudging on work hours, pilfering materials from the workplace, driving recklessly or well over the speed limit, disobeying parents and authorities, and . . . well, the examples could go on and on. They think it does not matter if no one sees.

In the illegitimate system of the fallen world, honoring authority is not a high priority. In our kingdom—the redemptive, governmental system of God—*disobedience separates us from the King*. The flow of blessings that follow obedience to our King and His government is broken, and we cannot receive from Him the things He wants to give us. In rebelling against God, we unknowingly build up the illegitimate authority of the kingdom of darkness.

God came to Earth as Jesus to regain the authority humanity had lost to Satan. After Jesus died on the cross, He went to hell and routed the enemy. He overcame death and gave the keys of the kingdom, the opportunity for dominion, back to those who believe in Him and are in relationship with Him. This is the restoration of the covenant—the relationship we lost through our disobedience. Access to authority God had originally given human beings was restored.

Jesus's purpose was to redeem us from the bondage of sin—buy us back from sin's claims—and to restore our relationship with God. But listen to what Paul tells the believers in Rome:

> *I'm so happy when I think of you, because everyone knows the testimony of your deep commitment of faith. So I want you to become scholars of all that is good and beautiful, and stay pure and innocent when it comes to evil. And the God of peace will swiftly pound Satan to a pulp under your feet! And the wonderful favor of our Lord Jesus will surround you.*
>
> —Romans 16:19-20 (TPT)

Paul only mentions Satan once in the book of Romans—and tells us that the enemy is doomed. We are strangers and foreigners on Earth as we live in the false kingdom. Our true citizenship and all our provision is from a country whose government is not made by human beings. Now, we are in right relationship with God. We, citizens of the kingdom of God, are not dependent on any other source for our needs. Furthermore, though we endure battles here on Earth, we know that in the end, Jesus wins the war against Satan.

The King's plans for us are for good; He promises us a hope and a future. We are given the authority to tread on serpents and scorpions and all other power of this defeated enemy. Satan is beneath our feet, and we can crush his head with our heels. We can be confident in the fact that our King who is living and working in and through us is greater than all the forces of darkness that are operating in the world today. Lesser authority always yields to greater authority, and there is no greater authority than our God. He has given us authority over the kingdom of darkness, and it must yield. It is not optional.

God provided a system. His redemptive government was delivered to the earth so we could operate in His authority and live with the dominion He originally assigned to us. We have seen that Jesus taught His followers to pray for His kingdom to come on earth, just as it is in heaven (Matthew 6:10). He also instructed them to pray that His will would be done on earth, just as it is in heaven.

Jesus very clearly declared that His government has already arrived on Earth. He brought His government with Him, comparing it to a small seed that grows into a big tree. The kingdom is everlasting and will eventually smash all other kingdoms of the world into nothingness (Daniel 2:44). This is sure and this is certain.

Jesus also clearly declared that He has placed His government inside of everyone who believes. Wherever a believer goes, so does the government and the authority of God. It is ready for our use and our engagement. It is like your passport—going wherever you travel and identifying you as a citizen of your country.

To clarify, God's kingdom has not *fully* come, but what is here is already stronger and more powerful than anything the kingdom of darkness has on the earth. If the kingdom had already fully come, Jesus would not have also told His followers to pray that it would come on earth as it is in heaven. It is clear from what we see around us and the headlines we read every day that though God's kingdom is here, it is not fully activated, engaged, or employed.

You may be wondering why God's kingdom has not yet fully come (a great question). Adam and Eve violated the original covenant, then for millennia God gave His people chances to restore it. Humanity chose not to do so, so Jesus had to come. Until Jesus returns, however, the *full* manifestation of God's kingdom will not be complete. Still, His kingdom that has already come is more powerful than anything on the earth now … we can walk and operate in the authority of His government here and now.

I recently re-watched the classic film *Bridge on the River Kwai*, directed by the great David Lean and starring William Holden and the inimitable Alec Guinness (yes, the same actor who brought us Obi Won Kenobi). In the film, Guinness plays Colonel Nicholson, the commanding officer of a group of British soldiers who have been captured by the Japanese. Despite the brutality and abuses suffered in the prison camp, Guinness demands a high standard of discipline from his soldiers. Major Saito, the Japanese camp commander, keeps insisting that the British are "prisoners rather than soldiers."

When one of Nicholson's junior officers, Major Clipton, pleads with him to give in to some of Saito's demands, Nicholson says, "One day the war will be over. And I hope that the people that use this bridge in years to come will remember how it was built and who built it. Not a gang of slaves but soldiers, British soldiers, Clipton, even in captivity."

This is a profound and relevant statement for us today: we are citizens of God's kingdom (Philippians 3:20), not slaves in the enemy's camp. While this present world seems in chaos and far from God, we can live within the boundaries of His governmental system. Because of our identity as citizens (rather than slaves), we can live today in the power and in the glory of His kingdom.

In the Japanese prison camp, Nicholson's men were able to remain disciplined and unified because they saw themselves as soldiers, not slaves. And so it is with us. The system of government God delivered to Earth is the law of the spirit of life in Christ Jesus (Romans 8:2), and it delivers believers from the law of sin and death under which this world operates.

If we want to know the disciplines and dynamics of the kingdom of God, we will find them clearly defined in the Word—the "Constitution" of His and our kingdom. The Scriptures are the values, the principles, and the established precedents by which we agree to govern ourselves. The Scriptures are our Constitution. They are comprehensive, and they cover every situation, each circumstance, and all the relationships we ever may encounter. Over the next few chapters, we will explore how to live out these principles relationally and experientially. They are the keys to the kind of life that everyone is looking for.

Knowledge That Makes a Difference

For all of human history, we have relentlessly sought the knowledge that will make a genuine difference in our ability to direct our own lives. Despite all the knowledge collected in all the books ever written, we still face the same obstacles: feeling helpless, deadly diseases, natural disasters, droughts, famines, the decisions of others—anything any outside force can impose upon us.

We crave the ability to control our own lives and their outcomes. After all, that is the exact temptation the serpent leveled at Eve when he said, "God knows that your eyes will be opened as soon as you eat it, and you will be like God, knowing both good and evil" (Genesis 3:5). Again, Jesus gave us two choices: the narrow road or the broad one. The first is the pathway of His kingdom, while the second is the road to destruction.

That age-old desire to wrest control away from the Lord has led many to attempt to become their own god. We see it every day on our news feeds—people desperately attempting to direct and manipulate the world around them to enforce their own agendas. But the result always seems to be hopelessness. We seem to be nothing more than dust in the wind, as some philosophies suggest, or victims to the unyielding tsunami of life that changes its path for no one. In fact, after the Fall, God told Adam and Eve that because of the curse in the Garden, they would "return to the ground, for out of it you were taken; for dust you are, and to dust you shall return" (Genesis 3:19).

We are constantly looking for some sense of influence, and we have tried numerous methods to obtain it. These age-old attempts include:

> **Religion**. Mankind's attempt to describe and explain God results in numerous methods for approaching Him, serving Him, and worshiping Him. That is why the spiritual landscape of this world is filled with major religions and their multitude of branches, denominations, and spin-off cults. There are literally tens of thousands of groups who believe they have discovered "the

way" to God through their belief system, practices, rules, and methods of worship.

Most religions have a standard of conduct and behavior for the ultimate purpose of getting to heaven or wherever God is said to live. Most adherents of any given religion find their practices to be ineffective for many of the daily experiences of their lives. The result may be either a theoretical belief system that has little practical application or disillusionment about how beliefs relate to the here-and-now. This is one reason Jesus remarked about people who worship God in vain and teach the commandments of man as if they are God's (Mark 7:7-9). Religion gives us a sense of moving toward God but without making a real connection with Him.

Power, influence, and fame. Many people have little regard for religion but seek fulfillment and control through power and position. They believe that the resulting influence will make them feel complete. They may seek power politically, financially, socially, or through becoming famous and influential, but in every case their goal is control—over their own lives, at least, and frequently over the lives of others.
Unfortunately, the road to the top becomes very narrow. They find very few peers and even fewer friends as they move up, resulting in feelings of loneliness and isolation. Their inability to be pleased or satisfied can lead to callousness and even ruthlessness. Often, they see

themselves in a no-win situation, unable to please everyone or anyone, and inevitably criticized by someone no matter what they do. They sometimes find themselves unappreciated and unable to appreciate others.

Alcohol, drugs, and sex. Sensual stimulants give momentary pleasure or fulfillment, but they dull the senses, over time, rather than enhance them. The amount of stimulation required to achieve the desired results increases with each use, creating perfect conditions for addiction and self-destruction. The senses exposed to artificial or immoral stimuli become dulled, weakened, impaired, and often unresponsive to normal activity.

Sexual sin—extra-marital (i.e., adultery or fornication) or homosexual sex—destroys human beings spiritually and emotionally from within, much like cancer physically destroys the body. God has given us clear boundaries for sexual relationships; He designed it for the marriage relationship. Sexual activity outside of marriage is harmful. Because the effects are not as immediately visible as those of alcohol and drugs, many people think nearly every sexual behavior is morally neutral and harmless.

The emotional and psychological damage of using sexuality in ways other than how God intended is just as real. Some generations have developed cultures that are prone to these activities. Not only do these behaviors damage an individual from within, but they also damage a society from within. Every great nation in history that developed a distorted view of sex began to erode and eventually collapsed. The Roman Empire in its latter stages is well chronicled in this way.

Wealth. There is nothing wrong with money; it is not inherently bad. In fact, it is a necessity of life in the earth realm as the means by which we buy what we need to survive. Without money, life on Earth becomes very challenging. Money is simply a commodity, a medium of exchange that is used for commerce.

Many people, however, use money as a means to power, control, and security. Money is the currency of the kingdom of darkness. Humanity's desire to possess more of it becomes an obsession of greater priority than deeper, more meaningful aspects of life—like relationships. We cannot be defined as successful simply by having great sums of money, nor can we be labeled a failure by the lack of it. Many people with material possessions fail in other areas of life, and many people struggling financially succeed in life. In and of itself, money has no value at all. Using money properly as a currency and medium of exchange in fulfillment of the universal laws of the kingdom—according to God's plan and in keeping with His purposes—is what determines its value. And using it properly involves using it for the good of others.

God provides and allows us to have money to meet our needs and to help others who have need. There are two kinds of people: givers and takers. I believe most people become takers because they do not understand the purpose and the plan for money. We spend much of our lives earning a living and gathering money. There is nothing wrong with that in and of itself.

But when we realize money is just a tool, a means to bless our families and those around us, giving becomes a natural result of earning. Unfortunately, however, many people do not have a plan for giving. If your earning plan does not fulfill your giving plan, you are pursuing the wrong kingdom. Money is a vital resource and gives us great opportunities to invest in the advancement of God's kingdom.

A tithe given at church can easily become nothing more than a tip or a tax given to God—an obligation to comply with before we spend the rest however we desire. Giving freely, when it comes from a truly generous motive and not simply as an obligation, opens doors that nothing else will open. It is part of the design and purpose of money.

Talents and special abilities. The attempt to control and determine the course of life is often expressed through talents and special abilities. Too many gifted people use their abilities to feed their own self-esteem and gather possessions for themselves. They forget their responsibility to humanity, and they miss opportunities to let their behavior and conduct be positive examples for others. Talents and gifts, whether musical, artistic, athletic, intellectual, scientific, educational, medical, or otherwise provide a significant reward when used properly and managed well.

Beauty and charm. In this era of technology and medicine, there seems to be nothing on the human body that cannot be altered. Nearly fifteen million cosmetic surgical procedures are performed in the U.S., annually. In 2020, the country was in a pandemic, the number of home foreclosures was rising alarmingly, and unemployment was a significant problem.[11] Not many people had disposable income, but apparently quite a few found money for cosmetic surgery. In fact, the statistics point to a global obsession with physical appearance.

The fact is, with time, physical beauty inevitably fades. To use beauty as an established measure of self-worth, rather than bringing it into submission to more meaningful and important aspects of life, is a plan doomed to fail. When a person's sense of worth is tied up in how good they look, what happens to their worth when outward beauty fades? Overvaluing appearance always results in pain.

The laws of conduct and behavior in God's government will create a society in which beauty is admired and appreciated but not over-valued. There is nothing wrong with beauty; God created it. But there *is* something wrong with letting it shape your identity, using it to find fulfillment, or allowing it to exert a sense of control over your life.

Government. The governments of this world are not the government of God. They do not represent God nor His way of doing and being right. They are the false governments whose king is the defeated Satan. They compete with the government of God for power, authority, and control of humanity. If humanity recognized and honored the government of God, there would be no need for civil government. The governments of this world pass laws that they are supposed to adhere to; however, what is legal very often conflicts with what is right or moral. Justice, equality, and fairness cannot be found in the governments of this world. These qualities can only be found in the kingdom government of our God.

Universal Dynamics of the Kingdom

The approaches listed above seem to be the primary methods through which humans attempt to find the kind of influence over their lives they desire, and there are certainly more. Ultimately, none of the above pursuits or efforts will deliver the happiness, peace, and sense of control that we seek. They will fail because the universal dynamics and systems of the kingdom are real. They are sure, certain, and eternal.

Laws/dynamics of conduct have inevitable outcomes, just as physical laws do. We can choose whether to obey the dynamics God has given us in His Word, but we cannot choose alternate consequences. The outcomes are results of their preceding actions. For example, you can ignore warnings that hiking a certain canyon requires ropes and basic climbing skills. Fast forward to the day when you choose to ignore the physical dynamics of that steep canyon and need to be airlifted with a broken leg by a medical helicopter. Outcome, indeed, followed action.

A casual survey of history or even personal experience will provide enough evidence to demonstrate that behavioral dynamics have certain consequences. We have seen what happens when someone lives with anger, unforgiveness, pride, dishonesty, immorality, and irresponsibility. They reap negative consequences, often blaming God or others for their outcomes. The outcomes of the lives of those who do not recognize the impact of their disobedience are chronicles of tragedy.

We have also seen what happens when someone lives with patience, forgiveness, humility, honesty, morality, and responsibility. They may not be immune to hardships, but their lives are built on a solid foundation, and they are able to weather any storm. They reap many benefits and blessings.

This is not a religious exercise. When we experience the painful results of trying to defy the law of gravity, it is not a religious experience. Dynamics, like gravity, inertia, and relativity do not work because we believe them. They work because they are principles of design that are absolute, and they are true. The example of the canyon fits here—whether we believe rope is needed to rappel a near-vertical cliff face is irrelevant. It is true regardless of what we believe. It is the same way with the dynamics of God's redemptive governance agreement. Whether we believe them or not, we will find them effective in our lives. If we choose to defy them, we will reap negative consequences. If we seek to live by them, we will experience the fruit of our obedience.

Dynamics Versus Laws

In the introduction, we discussed the difference between dynamics and laws. It is critical to point out here that God's redemptive eternal kingdom is guided by dynamics that have set outcomes. They are God-breathed, life-giving, and enduring. His love is one such dynamic, as is His grace. They never change; they never diminish.

When we invite the Father of Lights to guide us, He will. There is no shifting shadow or doubt of that dynamic. It is fixed and immune to culture or opinion. In contrast, if we seek the advice of the world, we will get one thousand opinions, all varying by degrees. The world gives sets of rules—laws—that shift, alter, and change depending upon the winds of culture and society.

For example, if you ask the typical person on the street how to get to heaven, what advice would they give? The answer, of course, is, "It depends on the person I am asking." And that is exactly the point. You will get the same result when you ask how each major world religion would answer the heaven question—a plethora of answers.

But what is God's answer to that question? There is no shifting shadow—the Word is clear when Jesus says, "I am the way, the truth, and the life. No one can come to the Father except through me" (John 14:6). He also tells us that "unless you are born again, you cannot see the Kingdom of God" (John 3:3). And to make things even clearer, He adds that "no one can enter the Kingdom of God without being born of water and the Spirit" (John 3:5).

If we lived within God's design and under the parameters of His system, we would each self-govern, and there would be no need for civil government. When we understand that there are universal dynamics, values, principles, and established precedents that govern our relationships and the outcomes of our lives, we are on the way toward self-government.

If we research, study, and rehearse these laws to the point of internalizing them, and if we allow our conduct and behavior to be managed by them, we will never need civil laws. Though this is how we were originally created to live, our disobedience put us in the position of needing to be constrained by external dynamics. As we are given a new nature and God's Spirit works within us, we are in the process of being transformed into the kind of people who are governed correctly from within.

The values, principles, and established precedents of God's redemptive government agreement address all of humanity's needs very specifically. There are universal dynamics for courage, character, vision, leadership, self-government, productivity, management, and more that can be taught effectively to anyone. Understanding these dynamics of values, principles, and established precedents, and then conducting our lives by their simple but profound truths, will provide us with the influence we have always searched for as we try to shape our desired outcomes.

The Nature of the Kingdom

The nature of God's kingdom—its highest values, priorities, characteristics, and ways of operation—can be discovered in the written Word, our Constitution. If we want a quick summary of how it should look in our lives, there are two pictures in the Scriptures that will show us all we need to know about living under His government.

1. Jesus as a Picture of the Kingdom

If we want to know the characteristics of the kingdom, we need look no further than the characteristics of the King. What was Jesus like? What did He do when He was on Earth? What attitudes did He respond to? What was His nature? What values did He hold? What were His highest priorities? How did He instruct His followers to live? When you take the time to think about these questions and attempt to answer them, you will begin to get a clear idea of the nature of God's plan as the redemptive government on the earth. Jesus is a perfect demonstration of a kingdom-first lifestyle.

Jesus emphasizes characteristics like humility, service, and generosity. He talks about values like hungering for righteousness, being peacemakers, and forgiving others. He operates in miraculous power, divine wisdom, and sacrificial love. These elements underscore the fact that right relationship is His way of doing and being right.

I like to use the word eternality—it's a seldom-used word, but it perfectly captures the essence of who He is and how His kingdom operates. Indeed, Jesus operates in eternality, on a level that transcends the time and space elements of our world. This is His kingdom. It is eternal and is available now on the earth.

Jesus is more interested in the heart, the spirit, and the eternal component of a person's makeup than in his or her appearance, status, or possessions. His purpose is to bless and to save, and He relentlessly seeks out those who are lost and in need of Him. This is not only the heart of the King; it is also the heart of the King's kingdom. This is the culture we live in as citizens under His government. This is eternality.

2. Heaven as a Picture of the Kingdom

If our prayer and mission is "on earth as it is in heaven," then we really need to know what life in heaven is like. We need to grasp the fact that the nature of God's government does not change between realms and dimensions. Kingdom character and attributes in one place (heavenly realms) will carry over to any other realm (the earthly realm). The culture of heaven is to be the culture of eternality we operate in, here, on earth.

What is heaven like? There is no disease, no strife, no pride, no bankruptcy, no sexual deviance or confusion, no futility, no family dysfunction— nothing of the obstacles and misfortunes that so often seem to overwhelm us here on Earth. Whatever challenges we face here, we do not need to resign ourselves to them as an acceptable part of our lives. If they are not part of the kingdom of heaven, they are not a part of our life on Earth. God has given us everything we need to overcome them.

These characteristics of God's kingdom are not yet fully manifest in our lives, which is why we need to understand which kingdom we belong to, then live according to the dynamics and the nature of that kingdom. It is clear from Scripture that we have wisdom that comes from God. Before the fall, Adam did not go to a university to learn about horticulture or zoology, but he was able to name every plant and animal and exercise authority over them. He had what we would call miraculous wisdom, though it was very natural to him.

The early church lived in the power of the kingdom. Today we call that miraculous, though it was normal for them at the time. When we learn to live in eternality according to the government of God, we will begin to experience the miraculous much more often than we do now.

Because His kingdom is like this, it is our inheritance as children of the King and citizens of His kingdom. It requires a life of faith (which is the substance, or reality, of what we hope for) and the absolute assurance of the tangibility of the things we cannot see with our Earth-born eyes (Hebrews 11:1). As we learn to see with the eyes of the Spirit as well as to believe, we will see and walk in the power of the kingdom. We will see the kingdom manifesting in our lives.

Seeking the Kingdom

Declare these words to yourself and about yourself often. The more you hear them come out of your mouth, the more they will shape your perceptions and become an integral part of who you are.

Whether you are gathered with others or reading alone, declare these truths out loud:

YOUR DECLARATIONS

KINGDOM SYSTEM RELATIONSHIP

- Father, in the name of Jesus (your name and your family members' names here), all of our heirs and all of our decedents forever, we declare that above all else, we seek the kingdom of God, Your plan, Your system and Your righteousness—Your way of doing things and of being right. We trust that as we are single-minded and wholehearted about your kingdom governance, all else will be added to us in abundance. (Matthew 6:33)
- We declare and believe that the time is fulfilled and Your Kingdom System has come. It is available to us and to anyone who enters into a living relationship with You, the living God. Anyone who fellowships with You, who spends time with You, and who submits to Your kingdom ways has access to the benefits of kingdom citizenship. We have changed the way we think and what we believe to experience the fullness of Your Kingdom System, both in relationship and in practical benefit. (Mark 1:15)

- We believe that the secrets of the Kingdom System of our God have been given to us. They are not hidden. You have revealed them to us, and we can fully live and function in Your redemptive, kingdom government here on the earth now. (Mark 4:11)
- We welcome the Kingdom System of our God into our lives as little children receive what is given to them. This is our dominion and our authority as given to us by Jesus, Himself. We are free to live as Kingdom System citizens while we function in this world. (Mark 10:15)
- We can, and do, fully experience the nature of Your Kingdom System in our lives. This includes knowing Your way of doing and being right, having peace that passes understanding, and being filled to overflowing with joy in the Holy Spirit. In this way, we will see God's power at work in us, through us, and around us. (Romans 14:7; 1 Corinthians 4:20)

All of the declarations found here, and many more, are available in the book Kingdom Activating Declarations by Charlie Lewis.

Visit www.ksam.net for this and other great resources.

CHAPTER 3

OUR ROLE IN THE KINGDOM

I love it when a plan comes together. We all do. When we are working on a project, aiming for a particular goal, facing a difficult challenge, or pursuing an important vision, it is extremely satisfying and refreshing when all the pieces begin to fit.

That is where I find myself today. I see pieces coming together and fitting into place in terms of my understanding of how His kingdom plan operates. I also see many people (whether living in a relationship with God or not) experiencing frustration and futility, trying to figure out how to make their plans come together. They are disappointed again and again. Whether we realize it or not, we are all on a journey to find truth and fulfillment in our relationship with our Creator.

We are either seeking God's plans and ways, or we are pursuing a substitute that takes the place of His plans. Either way, we are all looking for that missing key to "rightness." We want to do the right thing to arrive at the right place. For many, those attempts are not coming together well. I believe that for me and many others, it is all beginning to make sense.

I believe God is showing His plan for humanity and for the nations of this world. He has revealed His Word, and He is teaching truths not seen before. This is exciting! I am observing and seeing how He is doing this with many people—how He is creating the beginnings of a movement that will reshape how His people live and function in His kingdom. In fact, He is bringing His kingdom to the earth in unprecedented ways. He has told us that His plans for us are for good—for a hope and a future—and they really are. He is giving His people the understanding they need to live in His authority and power to see His kingdom come.

Come Kingdom Come: Keys to Seeing God's Kingdom Come

The following four observations are simple, but very significant, examples of the fact that God's people need to live in His authority and in His power to see His kingdom come:

1. Our Creator told us to reign on Earth. God told us that we have dominion over all the forces of the kingdom of darkness, and that we are to function from that position on the earth. This was one of the original assignments in Genesis. To have dominion over the earth did not simply mean to dominate the animal kingdom and use the earth's resources however we choose. Spiritual authority was embedded in our assignment, and we are called to be stewards of His beautiful creation, not abusers of it.

His plan for humankind was to forge a partnership with Him to establish His kingdom and to implement His government. Jesus restored that authority to us, but most Christians do not experience it. We do not understand that it is available or know how to use it. Our lack of understanding often manifests in either abusing or abdicating that authority, rather than stewarding it in a way that glorifies the Creator and respects His creation.

He gave us the power and authority to live victoriously, not only after we die and go to His heavenly realm but right here on Earth and right now in this age. His instructions are for now. He told us to occupy the earth and keep it under our control until He returns. Jesus would not have charged us to do something that He did not also enable and equip us to do. He has already given the instructions, and He has provided the way.

2. We are told that our Creator loves us individually. However, Revelation 15:4 says that He desires for all nations to come and to worship before Him. Believers throughout history have made great progress in their efforts to accomplish this goal (e.g., through evangelism, missions, etc.). Yet, in many areas we are losing ground. For example, here in the U.S., those who self-identify as "Christian" made up 63% of the U.S. population in 2021, down from 75% in 2011.[12]

3. The methods of the past have taken us only to a certain point, and many people have been redeemed. Most often, bringing people into the kingdom through a salvation message has not affected change in cultures and societies to then align with God's kingdom and its provisions.

Salvation, of course, is paramount, but the restoration aspect of the message has been overlooked. We have not included all the ingredients necessary to make disciples as Jesus instructed. Many churches and mission organizations of the past have focused on making converts but neglected to make disciples, ignoring Jesus's instructions to us. One of the last instructions that Jesus spoke before He ascended said it all:

> *Then Jesus came close to them and said, "All authority of the universe has been given to me. Now wherever you go, make disciples of all nations, baptizing them in the name of the Father, the Son, and the Holy Spirit.*
>
> —Matthew 28:18-19 (TPT)

Jesus' heart is for the nations. His commission and His charge to us is to make disciples. He does not simply say "tell them about Me" but purposefully uses the word "disciples," which infers instruction, mentorship, and long-term care and oversight. In today's church, however, many of those who have focused on making disciples have emphasized spiritual activities within the home and church, yet without impacting the workplace nor the various sectors and systems of commerce and society.

The kingdom is not a partial kingdom. The kingdom is everlasting and all-inclusive. In our culture, the word "totalitarian" has a negative connotation and refers to a restrictive, and even brutal, type of earthly government in which a single person has control. God's eternal kingdom, however, is totally perfect, totally loving, and totally redemptive. Totalitarianism that is not redemptive and begins in our eternal spirit does not and will not work. The kingdom is God's redemptive plan for governance, and it is totalitarian in the purest and best sense of the word.

While I strongly believe that what believers have done in bringing people into God's kingdom is vitally important, it is not enough. We have not taught people to live as kingdom citizens. Look at the disciples. All of them were laypeople (not clergy) who understood and operated in society and commerce. Peter was a fisherman (as were several others); Matthew was a tax collector; Luke was a physician; Simon was a Zealot (part of a Jewish religious sect), etc. Yet today, particularly in the West, we have drawn an invisible—and extra-biblical—line separating "professional" ministers from "everyday people."

What are we missing? I do not believe the answer to that question is complicated. We have overlooked the important because we have focused on the urgent. As a society, we have set our minds on the here-and-now—bills to pay, relationships to pursue or to fix, family, house, job, a new car . . . or whatever else is the pressing issue of the day. All of which is temporary.

As a result, the urgent has crowded out the important. We have chosen what is relative instead of what is absolute. Jesus said to seek first His kingdom and His way of doing and being right, and all else would be added to us (Matthew 6:33). We have not sought the kingdom of God first, above all else. I am convinced I see a way to focus on the kingdom as God's redemptive, all-inclusive, totalitarian system of government for everything.

4. Redeemed and restored humanity is told to go into the world and make disciples of those who have not received the understanding of the Creator's plan. Again, there is a difference between making converts and making disciples. Not only are we called to make disciples who love and follow the Lord, but those disciples are meant to bring heaven to earth—to be those who know how to be representatives of God's redemptive government on Earth.

Humanity is desperate for understanding and is groaning in pain and futility, looking for the manifestation of the evidence that sons and daughters of God exist. We are told that we are to be different, to add "salty" flavor to the world and provide the clarity of observable direction from our influence. Again, I am convinced I see a way.

Let us look at these observations.

Our premise is that our Creator loves us with a breadth and depth beyond measure. His love has no bounds and no restrictions. Because that is true according to His own Word, He would not charge us to do something without providing a method, means, system, or plan to carry it out. He would not make it too difficult to understand. This is a true and a reasonable assumption that can be proven by personal experience and by the ways He has dealt with people in Scripture and in history. He is the Father of Lights, and in Him is no shifting shadow (James 1:17). When people ask Him for wisdom, instruction, and guidance, He gives it.

That presents a bit of a dilemma.

One of our observations is that God has told us to reign on Earth. We are to exercise dominion and authority and power—not to be controlling and force people to do what God says, but to overcome evil and darkness so that God's kingdom of light covers the earth and is a blessing to all.

Humanity feels hopeless. People believe they are being swept along by circumstances, situations, and relationships that are out of their control. Oftentimes, they feel powerless to impact the outcomes of their lives. For the most part, we—including those of us in God's kingdom, feel more like victims than victors.

Much of our media reflects this pessimism and ethos of negativity. Many of our films and much of our music mimics this hopelessness. Check the "Billboard 100" to see how many song titles are uplifting. (I bet it is not higher than twenty percent of the songs.) At any given time, in any given era, the lyrics are somewhat sad, dealing with betrayal, loss, calamity, etc. There is also a wistful melancholy and propensity to look to tomorrow—someday, things might get better.

Interestingly, while the church's songs—hymns, modern worship songs, etc.—are typically positive in message, there is often a sense of "looking forward" to when we get to heaven. Then, things will be better. Then, we will be joyful and at peace. There is a lot of emphasis in Christian songs, and in our preaching and teaching, of being "not of this world" as well as what we can hope for "one day" when we are no longer here.

Much of the church is just waiting to be rescued because the earth is not our home, and we are not winning the battle. Can you relate to this? It is the sentiment of the old "Beam Me Up, Jesus" bumper sticker or, more recently, the NOTW (Not of This World) fashion line.

Context is everything, however. Consider Jesus' High Priestly Prayer in John 17:

> *I have given them your message and that is why the unbelieving world hates them. For their allegiance is no longer to this world because I am not of this world. I am not asking that you remove them from the world, but I ask that you guard their hearts from evil,*
>
> —John 17:14-15 (TPT)

Here we see Jesus praying to the Lord about humankind. It is an extraordinary glimpse into the relationship between Jesus and the Father, and it reveals much about Jesus' view of us as citizens of the kingdom. Jesus does not pray that we "hang on" or be "beamed up" until we die and go to heaven. Rather, He reveals our position as citizens of the kingdom:

1. He has given us His word. We have the instruction manual and our Constitution for

the "operating system" that is God's kingdom understood and engaged.

2. Because we are citizens of an eternal kingdom, and "not of this world," we will be hated (persecuted) just as Jesus was. But, as He did, we must love them.
3. He prays that we (His children) not be taken out of the world, but that we be "kept" from the evil one—protected and set apart from Satan, as salt and light.

It is interesting how Jesus' prayer is sometimes misinterpreted to mean, "Because we are not of this world, we need to withdraw from it, seal ourselves and our families away from the rest of humanity, and just 'ride out the storm' until we go to heaven or until Jesus returns (whichever comes first)."

Do you know "silo Christians" who have nothing to do with non-Christians or those who believe differently from them? Nowhere in Scripture does it say we are to withdraw from the world. The only time Jesus withdrew was to spend time with His Father in prayer (Luke 5:16). This is appropriate for us to do, too, but not what I am referring to. Temporary spiritual retreat is very different from serial isolation from the world. His kingdom is based on His love for us and, therefore, those who do not yet know Him. Indeed, He is not willing that any should perish but that all should come to repentance (2 Peter 3:9).

We are not called to be exiles on our own spiritual islands, but children of the eternal kingdom who tell others about His Son (salvation), then equip them to live victoriously (discipleship) in restoration.

Consider Jesus' words again … He does not pray for the Father to take us out of the world, but to keep us from Satan.

Have you ever noticed that the spiritual armor mentioned in Ephesians 6 is built for the front of the body (e.g., the breastplate of righteousness, shield of faith, sword of the Spirit)? In other words, we are equipped to move into the world—not to retreat from it—so we can confront and overcome the evil one and advance His kingdom.

Unfortunately, many have a false understanding, expecting Jesus to come back and establish an entirely different kingdom—"somewhere else"—that is completely based in the future tense. It is almost like we are on our tiptoes, maybe even jumping a little, hoping the rapture will take us away before the tribulation comes (whenever that happens to be).

From what Scripture tells us, is that reasonable? No. Jesus told us "on earth" as it is in heaven. This world, on this planet. He told us to be praying for his kingdom now, in this age, and to be using the authority He already gave us to see His kingdom come. It begins with embracing the truths in His Word that tell us who we are in Christ. He tells us over and over that we are His children, and that …

- We are more than conquerors (Romans 8:37)
- We are made to triumph in every situation (2 Corinthians 2:14)
- Greater is He who is in us than he who is in the world (1 John 4:4)
- We believe the promises that He sends us forth in with His power (Matthew 28:18-20)
- God will never leave us or forsake us (Deuteronomy 31:6; Hebrews 13:5)

- Jesus is with us always (Matthew 28:20)
- We have the keys of the kingdom, and whatever we bind on earth will be bound in heaven (Matthew 16:19)
- No weapon formed against us will prosper (Isaiah 54:17)
- We have the assurance that when we lay hands on the sick they will be healed (Mark 16:17-18)
- We can cast out demons, and we have authority over all the power of the enemy (Luke 10:19)
- Our shield of faith will quench every fiery dart of defeated Satan (Ephesians 6:16)
- When the enemy comes at us one way, he will be sent scattering in seven (Deuteronomy 28:7)

Do you ever ask yourself why your experience is not aligning with what you have been told in Scripture? I have come to believe that if my experience is not lining up with the agreement I have with my Creator, there is something I do not know about the agreement. After all, God is the same yesterday, today, and tomorrow; He has not moved. He is always ready to invite me into His presence. Nothing can keep me from Him or separate me from His blessings, except me. If my actual experience does not fit His description of what it is supposed to be, there must be something I do not know or that I am not doing. A faith adjustment is needed.

One of the most perplexing verses on this subject is found in Mark 11. Jesus passes by a fig tree looking for fruit and discovers that the tree is barren. Subsequently, he curses the tree. The next day the roots and the tree are withered, and Peter is surprised and points this out to Jesus.

> *Then Jesus said to the disciples, "Have faith in God. I tell you the truth, you can say to this mountain, 'May you be lifted up and thrown into the sea,' and it will happen. But you must really believe it will happen and have no doubt in your heart. I tell you, you can pray for anything, and if you believe that you've received it, it will be yours."*
>
> —Mark 11:22–24 (NLT)

For years, I think I was hung up on the thought of my faith being so strong that I could make mountains get up and move into the sea. After all, it sounds a bit outrageous. Recently, however, I have taken another perspective: Jesus was preparing His disciples to walk more boldly, particularly after His departure. He wanted to prepare them for situations in which they would need to take decisive authority in the spiritual realm to impact things in the natural world. In other words, He was training them to "have eyes to see" the eternal kingdom manifested in the earthly kingdom. And remember, there are only two spiritual kingdoms: the kingdom of God and Satan's counterfeit kingdom.

The Relationship Priority

God makes it clear that if we do not know something, we can ask and receive His wisdom. He will tell us in clear terms and will help us understand. Often, this is a matter of relationship. Our redemption gives us access to all the information about life we will ever need. Relationship is what opens the pipeline so communication and the resulting understanding functions properly, continually, and without a break in the flow.

God gave us an amazing gift—He made us in His own likeness. The reason He did so was so He could give us *another* gift, the gift of a relationship with Him. There are many kinds of relationships, some of them distant and formal and others very close and familiar.

God wants the kind of relationship with us that He first had with Adam and Eve in the garden, where we walk together in the cool of the evening and spend time talking with Him about the day. He wants us to experience an intimate connection with Him.

Relationship is not religion. Being religious does not require having a relationship with God. Religion only requires us to follow rules and stay within established parameters. Our Creator is not religious, and He does not accept religious acts. Worship is meant to be relational. If there is a contradiction between our experience in our daily lives and what God says is the true and authentic way to live, could it be because we have confused religion with relationship?

Every other religion on the face of the earth says God wants things *from people*: devotion, sacrifice, good works, piety, purity, etc. Christianity is the only world religion where God has things *for people*. He is not only our Savior; He is our Restorer and Redeemer. All three, but particularly the latter two, happen in relationship with Him. He is our provider. Again, unlike all other world religions, we do not earn His love or our salvation. It is a free gift to either receive or reject. Such free will is the essence of relationship.

There is nothing left for our Creator to do to provide redemption and restoration for humanity. He has already offered the sacrifice of His blood and died on our behalf. He has already entered the tomb, descended to hell, taken the keys of the kingdom, been resurrected out of the tomb, given the keys of the kingdom to His followers, and ascended to heaven to sit at the right hand of the Father. His work is complete. So, in all the major areas of our lives—spiritual, relational, emotional, intellectual, financial, health, family—what do we need to do to bring about a victorious, powerful, overcoming experience described by our Creator God?

The results in our lives are completely determined by our management of the relationship that is provided for us. We will explore how later in this book when we look at the law of the spirit of life in Christ Jesus (as presented to us in the New Testament), a completed work already established in heaven and on Earth. We can know that if we spend time with Him, He will cause our thoughts to align with His will. Then, our plans will be established and lead to success (Proverbs 16:3).

Will success be aligned with our preconceived notions? Not always. When we hear the word success, our cultural filters default to wealth and prosperity. Not God's. His definition of success—while it might involve earthly wealth for a believer—always points to the proliferation and advancement of His kingdom. Always.

Spiritual success has to do with God's destiny and plan for our lives. The more we align with Him and His will, and the more intimate our relationship with Him becomes, the more room He has to realize His destiny for us. If we follow His process—first believe, then see results and the evidence of what we believe—our major struggles with these questions will decrease, and our faith in His purpose and plan for us will increase.

Through our relationship with Him, He will help us develop our faith and confidence in Him and in His Word—His promise. We will see the outcome from the beginning. We will operate in eternality. We will not be dismayed by problematic situations, circumstances, and relationships. We will know Him and believe His promises, and we will call heaven to earth.

This kind of relationship is where all faith is generated. This is the engine room that generates the power to propel us down God's path.

Without relationship, there is no faith. To have this kind of relationship, there has to be fellowship. Our Creator is continually asking us to spend time with Him. He longs for us to set aside time just for Him. He wants us to desire fellowship with Him—to become ravenously hungry for it, in fact.

We may need, at first, to make a commitment to spend time with Him—in the beginning, even just a few minutes a day—but soon it becomes a desire and a passion. We will find that we can hardly function without it. Most importantly, that fellowship will open a line of communication that cannot be established any other way.

This may seem simple, but it is powerful and true. Spending time in fellowship with God will produce a relationship that will provide clear insight and direction on His purposes and plans for humanity. That knowledge and understanding will be so evident and simple that it will never again be difficult to see and understand those purposes and plans. When He speaks to us, we can rest assured it will happen. It may seem like a long time coming. There may be twists and turns along the way that we do not understand. But His purposes and promises will not be thwarted.

We see this repeatedly in Scripture. The promise to Abraham took years to fulfill, but Abraham did not stagger in his faith or doubt that God would accomplish it. Joseph's dreams took years to fulfill; Moses' calling was not realized for decades; and David stepped into the kingship only after a long, difficult journey.

When we spend time in fellowship with God, we can endure these processes. Our relationship will cause us to recognize His voice, and we will not want to follow the voice of another. This may not happen overnight. At first, it is hard to drown out the static of the world. Again, start slow—five minutes or so—and quiet your heart before Him. Listen to Him speak to you in His "still, small voice." Some like to journal to capture the thoughts and images He may be speaking. Like any other discipline, over time it will get easier to block out the noise of the world and sit calmly and quietly at His feet.

During this time, we also roll our works completely upon Him. We commit and trust them completely to Him (Proverbs 16:3). We know His will and grow comfortable in it, knowing His ability and commitment to perform it.

Why, then, is there such inequity between what God says and what we experience? When Jesus came, He taught us everything we need to know for living in His kingdom. In one of those teachings about life and our daily needs, He said something very significant: we should seek the kingdom of God first, as a priority above all else (Matthew 6:33). That means seeking His way of doing things, His truth, and His way of being right. As we seek and find the kingdom, all the other things we need in life will be added to us. We do not seek them in and of themselves; they come to us as a byproduct of making our search for His kingdom the priority.

The kingdom of God was not a new subject for Jesus. He taught about it continually; it was His central theme during His ministry on Earth. In preparing the way for Jesus, John the Baptist preached that the kingdom was coming. Jesus taught the arrival of the kingdom from the beginning of His ministry.

Oddly, an emphasis on the reality of the kingdom did not continue after the earliest generations of His followers. It is not in the Apostles' Creed (written circa 180 AD), and it is not very prominent in the teachings of faith today. Neither is it a major emphasis in the doctrines of large organizations and denominations (at least, not in the U.S.). When it is discussed, it is often in terms of a "one day," otherworldly kingdom that has little or no impact on our world or current situation. For far too many Christians, a present, "happening now" kingdom of God is a concept, not a reality.

Why did Jesus' major teaching become a peripheral concept? Maybe because the church, often under persecution in early generations, began to spiritualize the teachings of Jesus when they could not see many of them at work in the physical realm. Or perhaps it is because of the human tendency to turn living truth into lifeless religion—to systematize and ritualize our approach to God so that it becomes less than a relationship. Entire books could be written about why this happened, but we will leave those questions for another time. The point is that we have drifted away from one of Jesus' primary purposes for coming into the world, and we need to get back to it.

So, the two questions we need to ask ourselves today are:

1. What is the kingdom of God?
2. How does the kingdom operate? In other words, how do we make the kingdom the experience of our lives?

We already addressed the first question in the last chapter, though we will continue to explore the implications of it. The pressing question for us to consider now is the second question: how does the kingdom function in our lives? This knowledge and understanding directly impacts our ability to operate on Earth in power, authority, and dominion.

The Kingdom Is a Government

I want to revisit Daniel's interpretation of Nebuchadnezzar's dream in Daniel 2—the passage where he foretold the next few empires that would dominate the earth at that time. According to the dream and its interpretation, there would be a succession of kingdoms after Nebuchadnezzar's Babylonian Empire. After these kingdoms, another kingdom would come—an everlasting kingdom whose reign would not end.

Not only would this kingdom come on the earth, it would crush all other kingdoms and consume them (Daniel 2:44). It would not end or be left to others, as all previous kingdoms had been. In other words, this kingdom would be fundamentally different from any kingdom the earth would ever know.

Subsequent history showed that Daniel prophesized that after the Babylonians would come the Medio-Persian Empire, the Greek Empire, and then the Roman Empire. All these kingdoms operated under a system of laws and disciplines of government. These governments required obedience and support from their citizens, who in turn received benefits from their respective governments.

What about the kingdom that would come during the reign of the Roman Empire? Daniel said its government would come on the earth. In fact, it would become a great mountain and fill the earth (Daniel 2:35). It would not be created by human hands, and this is important. This kingdom would be more powerful than any other human government.

In retrospect, it is easy to see that Daniel is talking about the kingdom of God that Jesus brought with Him during the time of the Roman Empire. Why has that kingdom not consumed all other kingdoms, as Daniel prophesied? Why do believers today continue to insist that this kingdom is coming one day in heaven? That it is not so much a kingdom that is coming to Earth, as it is a kingdom that we will travel to when we leave Earth? Or, if it is coming to Earth, that it is coming "one day" when Jesus returns—which is long after the Roman Empire that followed the Greek, Persian, and Babylonian empires? Why is there so much discrepancy between Daniel's prophecy and our modern understanding of the kingdom of God?

Throughout the centuries, God's people have lived with quite a few misconceptions of His kingdom. When Jesus brought the government of heaven to Earth, it did not appear as many believed it would. It did not come with a visible throne, army, or governmental houses for senators or parliaments. Isaiah prophesied that the government would be upon the Messiah's shoulders when He came (Isaiah 9:6), and John the Baptist kept insisting that the kingdom was coming (Matthew 3:2). Jesus came and said that the kingdom of God is here (Mark 1:15). Present tense. He put the kingdom within us (Luke 17:21). But many, then and now, have missed it because the workings of the kingdom often do not fit our preconceived perceptions of governments in the earth realm.

We need to be reminded that the kingdom of God is not part of the governmental system of Earth. We do not establish His kingdom by passing the right laws and enforcing them in the lives of people who do not know Him or have a relationship with Him. His government is not a democracy, a republic, or any other form of government human beings have devised. It is a theocracy in which God is the ultimate authority. He is the King, and He establishes His reign through our lives as we bring the government of heaven to Earth to intervene in our situations, circumstances, and relationships.

It is extremely important to realize that the kingdom of darkness has no power over the reborn spirit—those who are born again, as Jesus described in John 3. For that matter, the kingdom of darkness cannot forcibly impact anyone who does not give permission to the agents of darkness. We must cede jurisdiction to the enemy. This happens when we fail to understand the kingdom of God as a "now" kingdom—when we fail to appropriate our authority and position as victors over the darkness.

Satan and his kingdom work through deception. They influence and create situations, circumstances, and relationships that make challenges appear insurmountable and inevitable. Still, Satan's kingdom does not have authority or power unless we give them access. We have too often yielded authority and given permission because we did not know that we had power over the works of the kingdom of darkness. We did not know how to use the tools God the Father has delivered to us as citizens in His kingdom. As it says in Luke 10:19, we have authority over all the powers of the enemy.

It helps to remember that these are fallen creatures—and that there are two thirds more angels of light than there are angels of darkness. As well, when Jesus tells us we have authority over demons, He means exactly that: His blood is far more powerful than anything the enemy can muster. We must access that power, invoke the name of Jesus, and serve eviction notices to any demonic forces coming against us. (Again, some wonderful books have been written on this subject; I encourage you to pursue them.)

Citizens have rights under the government of their kingdom. Their safety, well being, prosperity, protection, and opportunities are the sole responsibility of the king, who must provide an atmosphere where his citizens can prosper and enjoy health. Citizens are not free to act indiscriminately without regard to the government of the kingdom. They have rights, privileges, and responsibilities when they do what is right. The king allows them the right to choose how they will live within the parameters of his reign.

The king decides the laws, but they must be fair and reasonable, not onerous or overbearing. A citizen can be in right standing with the king by knowing the dynamics of the kingdom and following his conduct of behavior. Right standing entitles citizens to full kingdom benefits. To enjoy the benefits of the kingdom, one must know the benefits provided by the king.

Our King tells His citizens throughout His Word how they should live to be in good standing and to receive the full benefits of the kingdom. Those benefits include complete and total peace, joy, love, redemption from the kingdom of darkness, and full restoration of the redemptive governmental relationship and benefits of the kingdom of light.

The words of our King are sure, steadfast, and eternal (Psalm 119:89, Isaiah 40:8, John 10:35). They cannot be voided. They accomplish what the King says they will accomplish (Isaiah 55:11). Our King tells us that His plans for us are for good, for a hope and for a future, and not for disaster (Jeremiah 29:11).

It is therefore time for the citizens of God's kingdom to stop living with misconceptions of what His kingdom is. The kingdom of God is the redemptive government of God, and we can be confident that it is operating on Earth, even now.

It is very important that we recognize this and begin to function within the government of God. As Jesus said, His kingdom rules over everything. The next step is ours: we can engage in the kingdom, employ its dynamics and principles, and use its authority. Lesser authority must always yield to greater authority. There is no greater authority than our God's authority. His government rules wherever His people implement it.

God and His Systems

If we look carefully, we will see that our Creator is a God of systems. That does not mean He can be systematized, that we live by formulas, or that we can reduce our relationship with Him to a set of principles. Not at all. He is very "out of the box," and every time we think we have put our finger on who He is, He shows us another view of Himself. His ways have always been unpredictable to the finite human mind; however, He has set ways of operating in place that form the context in which we live and move and have our being. He is a God of order and systems.

Think about it. Everything He has created operates within a system: the solar system, Earth's ecosystems, astrophysics, the life cycle, the human body, the various systems that work within the human body—all of these are amazing examples of systems that work together in an integrated whole and a determined order. For the earth to remain in balance or for the body to function properly, these systems must operate as designed.

The kingdom of God is the governmental system that God Himself, as Jesus Christ, delivered to Earth so that humanity could live and operate in the order, the power, the authority, and the dominion that He assigned to humanity. We are meant to be able to direct the affairs of our lives—not as our own gods, but as representatives of His will and His ways on the earth. Understanding this system is the missing piece for humanity to have the influence we are supposed to have over the outcomes we experience.

As a trained pilot, it is laughable to say I could have trained someone to fly a military craft—or any other type of airplane, for that matter—in an hour. Just like any multi-faceted tool or instrument (violin, piano, and guitar come to mind), it takes time, study, and practice to gain proficiency.

For example, writing a book is not an easy process. Before I had written my first book, I did not think it would be that difficult. I was wrong. Famous Russian novelist Leo Tolstoy said,

> "If you asked someone, 'Can you play the violin?' and he says, 'I do not know, I have not tried, perhaps I can,' you laugh at him. Whereas about writing, people always say: 'I do not know, I have not tried,' as though one had only to try and one would become a writer."[13]

Though our salvation is free for the asking and instantaneous, understanding and mastering the systems within God's kingdom takes time, patience, study, and practice. Just as we do not pick up a violin and instantly expect to play Mozart's Violin Concerto No. 3, we must study and apply the systems and principles of God's kingdom, using His Word as our source. This is a lifelong pursuit. As I mentioned earlier, here I am in my seventies, and I have never been so excited about what God is revealing to me.

Some call this lifelong process sanctification or the pursuit of holiness. It is the narrow path that Jesus talks about. It is living each day in prayerful submission to God's leading in every decision we make. We can actively discern, learn, and implement the systems of His kingdom. We do not have to be passively swept along by the current of lies perpetuated by our defeated adversary. Our Creator has provided access to the power we need for victory over those deceptions.

The tragedy is that we have long accepted Satan's lies because we do not know how God's kingdom works, nor do we understand how to appropriate His plans and processes into our lives. But I believe God's people are waking up to the truth that His kingdom is now, and that it is accessible on Earth. It is Jesus' mandate that we must tell everyone this good news of the Gospel of the kingdom and the governance system of God. Our Creator has given us a charge and the ability to perform it.

As I write the update for this book, I scan national and international headlines that point out the increasing gulf between God's eternal kingdom and the enemy's false kingdom. We have survived a pandemic, but in the process, it seems the church is allowing itself to be torn apart with division. It makes me think of the expression that Jesus is coming back for a Bride, not a harem. While I am all for a believer's involvement in the public square, including the support of godly officials, I believe many in His church have made political discourse—and division—an idol. The governments of the world, including our own, will not save us. Earthly governments cannot love—only God's eternal kingdom can. We must, first, focus on His kingdom—everything else becomes secondary to that.

The Scriptures are our written agreement for governance from God, filled from beginning to end with the dynamics and disciplines necessary to follow Him. They include every piece of instruction we need to obey God to walk experientially in relationship with Him in His kingdom government system. This is how we exercise the power and authority of dominion.

I once compiled a list of all the places in the Word—the covenants of Scripture—that contain instructions beginning with "if" and followed by "then" (see Appendix for a partial list). The printout was more than one hundred pages. God has given us numerous conditional promises and assurances: *if* we do a particular action or have a particular attitude, *then* we will experience the blessings and benefits of that action or attitude. There is always a discipline to be obeyed for every blessing to be received.

Much teaching today focuses on the benefits of the "thens" without mentioning the disciplines of the "ifs." Particularly in twenty-first century America, we fixate on the benefits of being a Christian—salvation, God's grace and victory—but we circumvent what His Word says about discipline, sacrifice, suffering, and loss. In other words, our expectations of His kingdom are unrealistic and incomplete, leaving us confused and vulnerable to the seemingly "quick fixes" that the enemy uses to tempt us.

Could that be why we appear powerless in our battles with the already defeated foes from the kingdom of darkness? We declare our position of victory without having been taught the discipline that activates it and makes it work in our lives. This would be the equivalent of taking fresh army recruits and teaching them victory songs, but giving them zero military training, and then sending them into battle. Just because they understand the concept of victory does not mean they know how to secure their victory. Similarly, we end up defeated by an enemy that has already been defeated himself, and we wonder why God's Word did not prove "true" for us.

That was one of the laments of Israel during the days of the prophet Micah. They executed all the right mechanics. They performed sacrifices, said the right prayers, and attended the right festivals and rituals. Still, God was not accepting any of it. They did not know what to do. But Micah reminded them they already knew because God had already told them:

> *No, O people, the Lord has told you what is good, and this is what he requires of you: to do what is right, to love mercy, and to walk humbly with your God.*
>
> —Micah 6:8

Discipline and obedience were necessary to activate the blessing of God in their lives.

One reason we have missed this is because of our emphasis on the doctrine of justification by faith alone. We are saved not because of our works but because of what Jesus did for us. That is a true statement that we cannot compromise. Yet, in the process of not compromising, we have developed a strong aversion to anything that looks like "legalism." There are good reasons for that—we do not receive salvation by our self-effort, and our relationship with God is much more than "dos" and "do nots."

In our aversion to any hint of legalism, however, we have distanced ourselves from the truth that God set certain universal systems and dynamics in place that are still in effect. When we ignore them or try to get around them, it is like trying to do whatever we want on a computer without any regard for the "operating system." It will not work. Again, it is like an airplane with no fuel or a boat with no rudder. You can try to get where you want to go, but it is not going to happen.

Here is another way to look at it: try to get from one place to another without regard for the physical dynamics of transportation. No matter what we try, we still must function within a system governed by the physical dynamics of gravity, mass, velocity, momentum, aerodynamics, and so on.

We learned this very quickly in Viet Nam. The stage field I was in charge of was tucked right up against the border with Cambodia. As soon as you took off from the air strip, you could count to five and be over the border. All the laws of aerodynamics came into play to make that hard banking maneuver to stay on the right side of the border.

We can decry these dynamics and claim they are "legalistic," but we will still be human and exist just as we did before. In other words, just because we do not like a certain principle or universal dynamic does not mean it has changed or does not work. In my pilots' case, they could complain that the Cambodian border was too close, but that did not change the reality of the situation.

The principle here is that we will not get from one place to another unless we follow basic laws and principles. The car will not drive itself. We cannot walk if we do not get off the couch. The bus will not pick us up unless we wait at the stop. Such unrealistic expectations will leave us frustrated by the fact that we remain subjected to an environmental system that limits what we want to do.

Likewise, if we ignore the systems God has put in place for how we are to function spiritually, relationally, volitionally, and all other ways in this world; we will still be His children and have an eternal relationship with Him. Though that truth will not change, we will not be able to accomplish all He wants us to accomplish. We will not move from one place to another in the kingdom, at least not without getting extremely frustrated and encountering unnecessary challenges along the way.

The fact is that we cannot simply follow the dynamics without the relationship. The religious leaders of Jesus' day did that, and they did not experience the blessings of the government of God in their lives. They lived by the words about His system without having the dynamics in their heart. On the other hand, we cannot live by the relationship and expect it to have no outward, practical implications for our lives. It is impossible to love God yet have no appetite for His instructions. That is like saying, "I want to be in a close relationship with You, but I am not really interested in what You say or what You want me to do." If we want to exercise the power, authority, and dominion we have been given, it needs to be both: the relationship and the instructions. They cannot be separated. I have often considered when I am in the hereafter and when our Creator God shows me what His plans were for me in the earth realm, I did not want them to be far above what I actually did.

It is true that when we become Christians, we "exchange lives" with Jesus. We give Him our lives, and we accept His death and resurrection for ourselves. It is His righteousness working within us, and we depend on His works as counting for our own. God gives us that substitute (or substitutional) life—the life of His Son within us. His works accomplish righteousness in His kingdom. If we want to know the blessings of that righteousness as our actual experience, our actions and attitudes will need to conform to His righteousness working within us. As Scripture tells us, we need to become in practice who He says we really are. The Scriptures call that conforming to His image. As we do that, we begin to experience both the "ifs" and the "thens" of His covenant with us.

There is a most interesting phrase in Jesus' instructions to us about seeking the kingdom of God and His righteousness first. The *Amplified Classic* version of the Scriptures follows the instructions of Matthew 6:33 with an explanation of what it means to seek His righteousness. It means seeking His way of doing and being right or correct. *Those are the guidelines we operate under*. This must mean that there are many other ways we can choose to operate other than according to His way of doing and being right.

How do we know the difference? And how do we engage and operate in His way? In Romans 12:1-2, we are told not to think like the world thinks but to allow God to change the way we think to align with the way He thinks. We are to let our mind be renewed with the words of Scripture, our agreement with the Creator. Then, according to these directions, we will understand how simple and clear it is to see His will is for us and know what to do in every situation.

To recap how we begin to experience the government system of the kingdom in our lives:

- We are to seek God's redemptive kingdom governance system first—to operate in His way of doing and being right.

- We are to discern His way of doing things correctly.
- His way will often be completely opposite of what we have learned from our worldly culture.
- Practicing His principles may be uncomfortable at first.
- When we follow His way, it allows for everything we need on Earth to be provided.
- We will be free from the tyranny and oppression of the kingdom of darkness.
- We will begin to fulfill the dominion mandate and operate in power on Earth.

CHAPTER 4

THE CHARACTER OF A KINGDOM CITIZEN

Next to a lake house that we visit occasionally is the home of a young man in his early forties. Often when we visit, he is home with a different female companion. Usually, his lady friend has children with her—sometimes teenagers, sometimes younger. That does not keep the adults from staying up late, drinking heavily, and sleeping late the next day. They always wake up complaining about the way they feel because of the excesses from the night before.

I am always stirred by a nagging question: what are the children present in this situation learning by observing the adults around them? What impact is this behavior having on the life choices these kids will make one day? My spirit grieves at the thought. I am torn between a desire to rescue them and an urge to tell the adults about the love of the Father—the real, abiding love that offers a better choice, a better way. An experience that can cause you to wake up each day with peace, joy, contentment, and no headaches or nausea or ringing in the ears. God's design is for us to live in a way that causes us to feel good in body, mind, and spirit.

Unfortunately, however, that does not happen very often for many people.

Something is seriously wrong with our society's expectations for how people behave and what they experience. As a culture, we have low standards. The prevailing attitude of our day seems to be that morality and righteousness are outdated values that inhibit our freedom. What most people do not realize is that they are being enslaved by the consequences of not living according to His kingdom principles. In fact, the kingdom is a vague longing in most people's hearts, and few believe it is possible to enter into it.

I believe, however, that it is possible to see the kingdom of God manifested in the world around us. Praying and living for the kingdom to come "on earth as it is in heaven" is not only an invitation; it is our best choice for success in managing the outcomes of our lives. If that is our vision, then we need to seek God's kingdom, His system, and His plan first. God has given us everything we need to do that and, as a result, to experience the blessings and benefits of His kingdom.

What it means, however, is that we need to do some "adulting." By that, I mean we need to dig for deeper joys found in a life of obedience to His perfect ways, rather than caving in to base desires and wants for temporary—and ultimately enslaving—fixes. It means delaying gratification and learning to be patient. It means to wait for what God has (which is always better).

Many years ago, I read Pat Robertson's *The Secret Kingdom.* I was intrigued by the premise that there were established dynamics on the earth that humanity could operate within to achieve specific outcomes and prescribed results. I remember finishing the book and commenting out loud to myself, "Wouldn't it be nice if that were true?" It would be years before the Holy Spirit would stir my spirit to look deeper into the reality of that concept.

Character Matters

If we want to see the government of God implemented in the world around us, we first need to see it implemented within ourselves. We will talk about what we say and do in later chapters, but character is the source of our words and actions. Most people do not want to look within, but this is a key to seeing the kingdom of God manifest in our lives. It makes no sense to seek the kingdom of God and its righteousness outwardly without seeking it inwardly.

The kingdom-first life, from the beginning, is a life of character.

What is character? It is that ingredient in a person's makeup that determines his or her actions in any given situation, circumstance, or relationship. Not only do actions include decisions and behaviors, but also reactions like anger, bitterness, resentfulness, happiness, sadness, sympathy, forgiveness, vengefulness, or any other attitude. When Jesus taught us to seek the kingdom of God above all else, He was describing God's government in our spirit and our mind as well as in the world.

This seems to be one of the greatest needs in the world today. Almost everywhere we look, we see an absence of character. In every area of society—government, business, media, entertainment, family—we find more and more people displaying a lack of integrity and character. No longer can we trust government to do what is right. Government enacts laws for its citizens that government and its leaders do not obey. Good citizens in legislative and enforcement positions believe they can violate the laws they have sworn to uphold in the name of a "higher good."

No longer can we trust media to tell us the truth. Human beings have always been somewhat biased in their presentation of the truth, but news and reporting are becoming more and more blatantly slanted. In recent years, we have seen shocking levels of corruption among business and finance leaders. Laws, rights, and truth are very often perverted, and the public trust is consistently violated.

These are character issues. So is our morality. When someone looks at the opposite sex, is attracted physically or emotionally, and enters an extramarital relationship, lust is not really the main issue. The underlying problem is character. We know the difference between right and wrong, and many people choose to pursue what is wrong. Their character is not strong enough to say no. The fallout can be devastating, impacting other lives and generations to come.

How do we develop kingdom character? We seek His kingdom and His way of doing and being right. We lay down our own desires, even our own lives, and take up Christ's. You may be saying, "Yeah, but Charlie, you have been a Christian for a long time. I am not even sure how to do that." Fair enough. Do you know where character development starts? In our daily decisions.

Think about character building this way: Jesus' victory was not won on the cross, it was won in the Garden of Gethsemane. What do I mean by that? When Jesus was in the Garden, He was praying that God would give Him the strength to face the horrible pain of the crucifixion and all else to come. It is a very moving scene:

> *He went on a little farther and bowed with his face to the ground, praying, "My Father! If it possible, let this cup of suffering be taken away from me. Yet I want your will to be done, not mine."*
>
> —Matthew 26:39

Remember that Jesus was all God and all man. We sometimes forget—or think it is somehow blasphemous—to discuss Jesus' humanity. He was a flesh-and-blood man who could feel pain and sorrow, just like us. And He knew what was coming; the brutality of Roman crucifixion was well known. In fact, the Romans did not invent the practice, which can be traced back to the 6th century BC when the Persians practiced it widely. Jesus knew what He was getting Himself into.

Despite this, He turned to the Father and said, "Yet I want your will to be done, not mine." There in the cool night air, alone, Jesus secured our victory because He chose to do the right thing, even though He knew it would cost Him greatly. This is character. It is making the hard decision to do the right thing when no one else is looking. It is comforting to know that we have our greatest example of character in our Savior, Jesus.

Earlier, we discussed the narrow path that Jesus invites us to walk. While the broader path chooses expediency and convenience, the narrow path chooses character. It is about a thousand decisions you make every year. It means not cheating on your taxes when you know others are or telling the truth when you make a mistake. On the narrow path, Jesus promises that you will suffer; He guarantees you that you will be persecuted for standing up for Him.

What the enemy does not want you to know, however, is that on the kingdom's narrow pathway, the pain of this world produces patience; the suffering we endure builds our faith. This is the pathway to His destiny for your life. If you choose the broader road, you short-circuit His destiny for you. Is it easy? No. Is it hard to do the right thing? Oftentimes, yes.

But listen to what Paul says about when we decide to follow God's direction:

> *Now all discipline seems to be more pain than pleasure at the time, yet later it will produce a transformation of character, bringing a harvest of righteousness and peace to those who yield to it.*
>
> —Hebrews 12:11 (TPT)

Character begins with the very next decision you make. Especially those decisions that might otherwise tempt you to cut corners, lie, or cheat just a little because "everyone else is doing it." That is the definition of the broad road that leads to destruction. That is the highway that leads to spiritual death (at worst) and guilt and remorse (at least).

Our character becomes that internal warning light that tells us that the instant gratification of premarital sex is the poor choice versus waiting. The Holy Spirit is the One who guards that internal light; however, the Holy Spirit can only work to the capacity by which we allow Him. In other words, complete surrender brings Holy Spirit fullness. The more we decrease, the more He increases.

Kingdom character is not developed by being afraid of getting caught. The question is not whether we are going to do the right thing when others are looking. That would make it a matter of self-preservation instead of right and wrong—the difference between being upset you were caught versus remorseful for making the mistake in the first place.

Kingdom character means being able to walk into a room full of thousand-dollar bills stacked to the ceiling, knowing no one would ever notice if you took all you could carry, and walking out without having touched any of them. It is picking up that stack of bills that just fell out of a person's pocket walking ahead of you and calling out to them so you can return them. You do the right thing because you have chosen to be a kingdom-first person, because you do not desire anything more than being like your Father and honoring your relationship with Him.

Oftentimes, people—even those who believe in God—compromise their values and live without reference to Him. Many even arrogantly flaunt their lack of character with an "in your face" independence. Many children are born out of wedlock because their parents are casual about their commitments or reluctant to commit in the first place. This is not just a symptom of a changing culture; it is a sign of a serious loss of character and integrity in our society.

Our Creator is a God of covenant. He bases His relationships on His commitment and His faithfulness, and He wants His people to do the same. God honors those who keep their vows, "even when it hurts" (Psalm 15:4), and He hates divorce. He tells men to rejoice in the wife of their youth (Proverbs 5:18) and that our prayers can be hindered if we do not honor our wives (1 Peter 3:7). God does not change; He is reliable and constant. He keeps His covenants.

We all know many people—within and outside the church—who have been divorced. Character also leads us to not judge or condemn them but to look beyond whatever factors might have led them to divorce in the first place. We also know God-loving people who did not want to divorce, but their spouse chose to leave or was otherwise unrepentant in their behavior. This is where our own character—forged through intimacy and consistency with God—brings discernment rather than pharisaical judgment.

What are we telling our children when we are casual about matters of character? The young and impressionable are looking for the right way to live. They are looking for their moral compass and want to make right decisions. God created us with that desire. We long to do what is right and just and to live in a deep, abiding relationship with

Him. Somewhere deep inside of us, we long for purity and truth. Everyone does!

The prison inmate convicted of murder did not desire that outcome when he was a child. The crack addict on the street corner had very real dreams when they were six years old. When she was twelve years old, the white-collar investor did not imagine she would defraud her customers twenty years later. Somewhere along the way, however, too many people compromise their true longings and serve their own self-interests by cutting corners with their integrity. It often starts with a single decision—which then adds up to many wrong decisions and a pathway toward destruction.

Instead of demonstrating the nature of the God who is constant and never changes, our society has decided it is normal and expected to tell "white lies," experiment with our sexuality, fudge the numbers on our tax returns, and cheat to get a competitive advantage. The "religion of the day" is relativism, which is based on the premise that what is true for you is not necessarily true for me. "You do you," "be your own person," and "do it your own way" are slogans of our relativistic culture.

Another feature of relativism is that any wrong action does not matter if we do not get caught and if it does not really hurt anyone else. Our children get the message loud and clear: you cannot really trust anyone. How can you when everyone has a different definition of right and wrong, good and bad? Once we leave the narrow path of God's Word, we lose our moral compass, and chaos and confusion reign.

Fraud, relativism, casual sex, deception—these character flaws are so common in our society that we can become numb or accustomed to them. As a culture, we are collectively like the proverbial frog in the kettle of water, and we are slowly boiling to death. Without God as our moral compass—the One who course corrects and recalibrates our "true north" reading—we are highly susceptible to character failures.

A lack of character is very often a symptom of looking to something or someone other than God for our fulfillment. Think about it: we would not lie or manipulate or overstep our God-given bounds if we really trusted Him to provide for us, protect us, and fulfill us. We only choose wrong actions because we think we must take care of ourselves and get whatever we can get on our own. We take matters into our own hands and rely on our own resources. Such moves are driven by fear, which is not seated in God.

The results are both heartbreaking and tragic. We all know someone who comes to the end of their life brimming with regrets or estranged from all the people they once loved or who loved them. That decision to pursue five minutes of pleasure then harms you for the next five years or worse. The impulse to leave your spouse for a "shinier model" may feel good in the moment, but at what cost to your children—and your children's children?

Satan is predictable, yet humankind continues to fall for his same, evil tricks. When we focus on making one good decision at a time—day after day, year after year—we find that "doing the right thing" becomes easier. Resisting the devil becomes more and more possible. We build up our character; we strengthen ourselves in the Lord. We become more and more spiritually fit one decision at a time.

When we look to God for all of our needs, fully trusting Him to give all those things that are added to us when we first seek His kingdom, the path is cleared for us to pursue the character of the kingdom. There is no need to contradict God's character because He is the one who gives us everything we need! The scales no longer tip in the direction of giving in to temptation and sin because we have tasted of the Lord, and He is good.

This is how and why we can live with complete integrity. It is part of seeking first His kingdom and knowing that "all these things"—the provision and protection and contentment we need—will be given to us.

How to Attain Character

Character must be developed. It is not something you are born with. We all get to develop the character we want. Corruption, immorality, evil desires—these things do not just happen to us. We choose them by the decisions we make. Some people may have been through experiences and conditions that make it difficult for them to choose otherwise. We can suffer abuses and emotional wounds that manifest in some really ugly ways. But, ultimately, we are responsible for our choices. We can choose to pursue what is right and just.

That should go without explanation, but we live in an era in which personal responsibility is a foreign concept to many. Oftentimes, what we see are people screaming about their rights rather than about what is right, including their personal responsibility. We see many presenting to the world with a victim attitude rather than with the posture of victory in Christ.

People will sue for just about anything while ignoring their own responsibility in the situation. One high-profile example of that is the tobacco settlements: hundreds of millions of dollars given to people who willingly bought cigarettes, put them in their mouth, lit them up, and inhaled the smoke. They eventually experienced the consequences of their actions, but they received huge settlements from the tobacco companies that provided the cigarettes.

Cigarettes did not give them cancer; their own lack of self-discipline did. It is a character issue. Maybe the health warnings were not strong enough, but people knew for years that cigarette smoke was not good for them, yet they continued to smoke. It is convenient and trendy these days to deny personal responsibility for one's own actions.

A person who thinks his character is simply a product of his culture, his family situation, or his peers is very mistaken. The person who is passive, simply going with the flow of culture and doing whatever seems right at the time is also mistaken. We choose our character, one way or another, one decision at a time. Not choosing is a choice. Character development is not a random process; it is the result of the choices we make and the values we want to cling to.

Many people seem to believe having a strong sense of character and values is not very important. In today's culture, the thoughts and beliefs of the individual are valued over other external sets of beliefs or values. In this sense, individualism is relativism's cousin. This profound elevation of individualism causes many to think that their character is not subject to any higher laws of conduct or behavior other than their own beliefs and opinions. After all, when we are our own god, we make the rules.

And to question this fierce individualism is seen as taboo. A lot of people seem oblivious to the possibility that their character choices affect other people, and they do not realize that every individual's actions almost always affect the people around them. Character always has consequences, whether for good or bad.

Keys to Character Development

So, how can you develop character? Many people think it is just a matter of establishing the right habits, but that is behavior, not internal character. Character is a much deeper issue. Here are some specific steps you can take to let the kingdom of God come into your life:

1. Realize the importance of character. Our choices and actions are a product of our character, and actions create a force, an energy in and of themselves. They go to work on the designated outcome you choose. If character is what shapes your actions, it has a huge influence on how the kingdom manifests in your experience. Character is where your outcomes begin to be formed.

If we want to be kingdom-first people, we need to understand that the kingdom comes within us before it comes around us. There are dynamics of conduct and behavior that have outcomes. As mentioned in Chapter Two, laws are not bad; they are only an affront to the lawless. To those who are seeking God's kingdom above all else, they point us in the right direction.

2. Do not get the obedience of character and behavior confused with self-effort and legalism. This is not an issue of salvation or being born again. You do not obey the law to become a kingdom citizen. You follow kingdom dynamics because you are already a kingdom citizen if you believe in Christ. As kingdom citizens, we want to know both our responsibilities and our privileges. The two go together.

When we are born again, we become citizens of the kingdom. Most of us come into the kingdom, slam the door shut, and back up against it—never walking into the kingdom and experiencing it. We focus only on salvation and redemption, not on restoration. If we want to experience restoration, we simply must understand and engage the system of government that makes restoration possible. We need to live, think, and react within that system.

3. Learn to recognize and understand kingdom character. Look at Jesus as an example. Read God's descriptions of what a kingdom citizen looks like. Explore those if-then statements that God gives us in His Word. (See appendix for some examples.) Very often, the "ifs" are character issues. Find places in Scripture that identify God's expectations and instructions for His people. Micah 6:8 is a good example. We looked at it in the last chapter: "No, O people, the Lord has told you what is good, and this is what he requires of you: to do what is right, to love mercy, and to walk humbly with your God." That is the character of a kingdom citizen.

4. Ask for the help of the Holy Spirit. You cannot do this yourself. Inner transformation is something that happens only by God's power. Your inner transformation will greatly impact your outer world, so do not underestimate its importance. Do not think it is all up to you, either. Continually pray "your kingdom come in me as it is in heaven."

YOUR DECLARATIONS

THIS IS WHO YOU ARE

In order to live out your calling as a kingdom citizen, you cannot dwell on thoughts of your own weaknesses and faults. You are who God says you are, not what your past says about you, what others say about you, what the defeated Satan says about you, or what your own mistaken and negative thoughts say about you. Declare out loud who God says you are.

- **I am strong.** God gives power and strength to His people. (Psalm 68:35)
- **I am victorious.** Every child of God overcomes the world and achieves victory through faith. (1 John 5:4-5)
- **I am valued.** God bought me with a very high price. (1 Corinthians 6:20)
- **I am one of a kind and like no one else. I am unique.** God made every part of me, in all my intricate detail, and knit me together in my mother's womb. (Psalm 139:13)
- **I am God's workmanship.** God has made me a masterpiece and prepared good works for me to do. (Ephesians 2:10)

- **I am loved.** God loves His people and draws them close to Him with an everlasting, unfailing love. (Jeremiah 31:3)
- **I am important.** I am chosen, a royal priest and member of a holy nation, God's very own treasured possession. As a result, I show others the Goodness of God because He has called me out of darkness and into His marvelous light. (1 Peter 2:9)
- **I am clean and I am forgiven.** He has removed my sins as far as the east is from the west. (Psalm 103:12)
- **I am a new creation.** Anyone who belongs to Christ has become a new person. The old life is gone, and a new life has begun. (2 Corinthians 5:17)
- **I am protected.** God will not let me stumble. He who watches over me will not slumber. (Psalm 121:3)
- **I am empowered.** I can and I do all things through Christ who strengthens me. (Philippians 4:13)
- **I am chosen.** Jesus chose me and appointed me to go and to produce lasting fruit, so that the Father will give me whatever I ask for using His name. (John 15:16).
- **I am family.** I am not a stranger or foreigner to God's kingdom, but I am a citizen along with all of His holy people. I am a member of His family. (Ephesians 2:19)

All of the declarations found here, and many more, are available in the book Kingdom Activating Declarations by Charlie Lewis.

Visit www.ksam.net for this and other great resources.

CHAPTER 5

THE MIND OF A KINGDOM CITIZEN

Fran and I hit the ground running after I returned from Viet Nam. We were stationed in Fort Jackson, South Carolina, where I was the Company Commander of a Basic Training Company. My position of captain allowed us to enjoy the comfortable lifestyle of an officer's family, and it felt like things were starting to settle down for us.

But God had other plans.

Fran and I wanted God's will for our lives, and we prayed for that. We just did not expect God to answer the prayer in the way that He did.

The life of an army officer is one of hard work but also has nice benefits—formal dinners, parties, social events, and a lot of free time. Fran enjoyed it, as did I. We were young, in love, and excited about the future.

Then God spoke to my spirit in prayer one day—out of the blue—and told me that He wanted me to resign my position as an officer and return to Jacksonville to help my dad with our participation in the family's furniture businesses. Fran was not happy to hear that news, to say the least. But we did exactly that: we left a comfortable military life for a nice, small home in Jacksonville. We threw ourselves into the work of running the businesses while my dad focused more on ministry. The business prospered and became very successful.

We also became involved at a small church, working with the youth in one of the poorest areas of Jacksonville. We started with approximately six young people, but God blessed our efforts and within three years, we had grown to around 300 youth attending services almost every night. We did not consider ourselves charismatic, but God was doing a lot of miraculous things—people were being healed; many were Spirit-baptized, and others were delivered from addictions. We did not know a label for it—God was showing up, and it was beautiful. The testimonies of those teens would crush the hardest heart.

But God had other plans.

We were at our peak in Jacksonville with the church, the youth group, and our professions, but God started speaking in both of our spirits that it was time for us to leave.

Though it was very hard to say goodbye to the youth in Jacksonville, we felt called to start our own business in an entirely new city. After some research of various towns, we settled on Thomasville, a town of about 20,000 in southwestern Georgia.

This was before we had children, but still, our families thought we were crazy. Why leave a successful family business to start over in a new state and in a strange town? But we felt confident that we'd been called by God. Even though we had not yet discovered the key principles of God's kingdom on Earth "as it in heaven," we were moving in His kingdom path.

Placing the Kingdom First

Seeking first the kingdom of God and His righteousness begins with letting the kingdom live and thrive within us. Clearly that impacts our own lives, but how does it impact those around us? One simple word: demonstration. Even though Fran and I had zero training for "professional ministry," God honored our heart, and He moved powerfully through the Jacksonville youth group. That is not bragging; it is simply acknowledging that God was faithful when we invited Him into our circumstances. And through that time, He demonstrated His kingdom to those young people—many of whom came from lower-income, broken, or abusive homes.

The people God brings into our lives are not looking for religion. The world is already full of religions; we do not need any more. If religion were the answer, people searching for whatever is missing in their lives would go running to it. No, those who are desperate do not need a new philosophy or theory or approach to life.

People are looking for something that will truly impact their situation, their circumstance, or their relationships. They need to know how they can more effectively confront their challenges and their sense of feeling out of control. Whether their challenges are internal (dominating their thoughts, desires, and actions) or external (dominating their circumstances and relationships), they long for real answers.

Far too often, people who do not know Christ look at Jesus followers and see us battling the same struggles and challenges. Non-believers may see a better attitude or a wiser approach to dealing with those problems, but they are not seeing a lot of real solutions. Deep inside our spirit, we know this is not right. There is supposed to be a better experience with the Lord who promises victory and deliverance and success.

God does not promise that we will not face challenges and trials, but He does promise that we can overcome them. He gives provision for the healing of illnesses, the abundance that eliminates chronic lack, the strength and strategies that overcome enemies, and more. We must learn how to access these solutions and then demonstrate them to a watching world in need. Our experience needs to change.

In the Book of Acts, people noticed demonstrations of power among people who believed. That is how the good news spread. Demonstration proves reality. It is the verification of the existence of a belief that cannot be denied. The answer may be obscure, but it is not hidden. It is clearly presented, demonstrated, and verified. The one who longs for, hungers after, and searches persistently for the solutions and strategies of the kingdom will not be denied. The one who keeps on asking, knocking, and seeking will find kingdom answers.

Jesus, the greatest teacher, said those who recognize their need for help will receive the kingdom. As we have noted, Jesus taught about the kingdom more than any other subject. That was why He came to Earth: to deliver the kingdom, which is described as a relationship with a King. Jesus demonstrated the presence, power, and authority of the King by everything He said and did. He showed that He was bringing the kingdom into our midst and offering it to us, for us to implement and engage with.

Jesus not only gave us many teachings, but he also gave us many examples of how to see the kingdom. He showed us how to enter it, live in it, and experience its power. In the thirteenth chapter of the book of Matthew, Jesus provides eight kingdom characteristics for us to study. He says "the kingdom of heaven is like …"

- **A Sower of seeds:** verses 3-9 (an image of the people of the world and how only a few who hear the Word land in "fertile soil')
- **The wheat and the tares:** verses 24-30 (the kingdom will be "sifted," and those who are not of God will be cast into the flame)
- **The mustard seed:** verses 31-32 (faith that begins small can grow to be mighty in God's kingdom)

- **A bit of leaven:** verse 33 (our witness can affect an exponential number of people)
- **A treasure hidden in a field:** verse 44 (how no earthly wealth can compare to God's kingdom riches)
- **A pearl of great price:** verses 45-56 (recognizing the value of God's kingdom and giving everything to attain it)
- **A dragnet cast into the sea:** verses 47–50 (how the angels will gather all together and those who do not know Him will be cast into the flame)
- **Treasured things old and new:** verse 52 (mining the riches of God's kingdom to realize your destiny)

When Jesus came and announced that the kingdom was here, it was (and is). In other words, it had arrived on Earth. The paradox, however, is that the kingdom is partly present, and partly future. Think of the coronation of a king. Upon ascending the throne, that king's rule begins. But over the course of a king or queen's reign, much happens.

Look at the late Queen Elizabeth II of Great Britain, for example. She ascended the throne in 1952 as England emerged from the ashes of World War II. Who knew that in all of England's 1,000-year existence, the young queen—only twenty-seven when crowned—would reign for seventy years, longer than any other English monarch. Similarly, the beginning of the kingdom "on earth as it is in heaven" came with Jesus, has been present ever since, and will continue to grow and increase into the future.

And when Jesus brought the kingdom to Earth, He gave us the tools to use its spiritual, financial, physical, emotional, and relational benefits. He showed us how to make deposits into and withdrawals from the kingdom. Everything we could ever possibly need was prepared for us before the foundation of the world and was placed in the kingdom for us to access.

We do not have to earn these benefits. In fact, we cannot. We can never be good enough to deserve the kingdom. We are given access when we believe it and declare it out loud with our voice. We align ourselves with His purposes and plans and declare them to be correct and right—knowing, accepting, and believing that we will receive what has been provided for us by our Father. Jesus came to declare liberty and to set captives free; to make our experience one of power, not weakness or defeat; and to promise plans for good, not for disaster. He came to express His goodness through His kingdom.

How do we make this our reality? Not to oversimplify, but it only involves four steps. Commitment and perseverance will be required, but the kingdom promise can be our ongoing experience if we incorporate these four key truths into our lives:

1. We must know what God said we are to have and to experience.
2. We must allow God to turn that knowledge into a vision—the picture or understanding—of how we walk out this knowledge in our lives. Minute by minute, day by day, without exception, we translate this understanding into a vision of kingdom reality.
3. We must allow God to show us His plans—by His Word, His Spirit, His teachers, His prophets, His preachers, and His citizens—for the vision to

become our reality. It will become easy to know the will and plan of God that we can activate and perpetuate in our lives. How? He will create a hunger for the relationship that achieves the plan. The relationship will be our delight and our heart's desire.

4. We must allow His plans to become our plans. Our experience will be the reality of the results He promised. Then, our plans will be established, and we will succeed.

When this becomes our practice and pattern for living, we will possess and display what the hungry, desperate, lost world is searching for. This is the image and likeness of God in us, the body of Christ recreating the power of His presence, His Word, and His Spirit. That power that is in us through our relationship with the King is the key to victory over situations, circumstances, and relationships.

It is the presence of the kingdom lived out in our visible experience and delivered into every opportunity God presents. It will be birthed by God the Holy Spirit, with power, and it will be easily and readily identified with undeniable results.

Vision and the Dynamics of Thought

You may have noticed that the major emphasis in these four steps is what happens inside of us. We are seeking God's kingdom and looking to make it manifest in our lives and in our world, but the process from vision to fulfillment begins in our thought life. What are we conceiving? Are our thoughts filled with faith or doubts? Do our thoughts really matter?

In his 1902 essay "As a Man Thinketh," British philosopher and author James Allen wrote, "Men do not attract what they want but what they are." The title is taken from Proverbs 23:7— "For as he thinks in his heart, so is he." That is one of the reasons we discussed the importance of character as the first step in becoming kingdom-first people. Our thoughts are enormously important in seeing the kingdom come in our lives. What happens inside of us shapes what happens outside of us. I have included some of Allen's more powerful quotes below:

> A man is literally what he thinks, his character being the complete sum of all of his thoughts. (p. 7)

> The soul attracts that which it secretly harbors; that which it loves, and also that which it fears; it reaches the height of its cherished aspirations; it falls to the level of its unchastened desires, and circumstances are the means by which the soul receives its own. (p. 16)

> Men are anxious to improve their circumstances but are unwilling to improve themselves; they therefore remain bound. (p. 19)

> Cherish your visions. Cherish your ideals. Cherish the music that stirs your heart, the beauty that forms in your mind, the loveliness that drapes your purest thoughts, for out of them will grow all delightful conditions, all heavenly environment, of these, if you but remain true to them your world will at last be built. (p. 50)

Allen's premise is that what we are today is the sum of all our past thoughts.[1] What are thoughts, and where do they come from? They come from what we are exposed to, some of it by choice and some of it not. Our exposure comes mostly from what we see, hear, and read. We process information to organize it, make sense of it, understand it, and prepare to respond to it. Thoughts are how we accomplish this processing.

Many people assume their thoughts just happen, as though the pathways in their minds are random. Those pathways may seem that way, but they are really chosen. Once we see, hear, or read anything—or receive it through any other sensory perception—it is then our responsibility to examine and evaluate the information. This requires effort and action. Whatever the source of our exposure, all information should be examined and researched. Truth can stand the scrutiny. Untruth will always be exposed.

One of humanity's biggest questions is, "What is truth?" Where can we find it? How do we know what is true? For followers of Jesus, we have an infallible standard. He is the Truth, and His Word is the truth. These are reliable and dependable sources, absolutes that we can cling to as revelation from God Himself. This is where our understanding of the kingdom and our knowledge of God's promises and provisions come from.

We are in an ongoing relationship with God in which we continue to receive information about His purposes and plans for our lives. He gives us desires, dreams, visions, and directions that He invites us to experience. We are never at a place where we cannot see and hear from Him. When we make the effort and take the action necessary, His way becomes abundantly clear and easy to understand and follow.

Everyone has a multitude of thoughts on any given day, and they derive from many sources:

- The people we spend time with
- The words we meditate on
- What we are taught
- What we have absorbed in the media and through television and films
- What we have researched and studied

After we receive these sources of information it is critical that we ask:

- Where do our visions and intentions come from?
- Is what we have researched and determined to be true based on accurate, godly information?
- By whose standard do we determine truth? Ours or someone else's?
- Is it what God says by His Spirit and His Word?
- Have we seriously examined the source of our beliefs?

Whatever information we are putting into our mind is going to influence what is coming out of us. Good input equals good results. Bad input equals bad results. The best way to determine if we are operating with good or bad information is to notice the impact of our vision on our results. We will know our thoughts and visions by the fruit our lives produce.

Several of Jesus' teachings and parables—the parables of the talents and the minas, for example—emphasized the results His followers were able to deliver to Him. He determined whether servants and stewards were good or bad by the results they obtained. Apparently, results are important to God, so we cannot rationalize or excuse poor performance. While His love is unconditional, He is a God of excellence, and we should deliver no less than our best.

We can recognize the beliefs that create our vision or perception and change both to be consistent with what God says in His Word. This aligns us with the system God delivered to Earth in Jesus and provides the way for humanity to live in dominion and authority. The kingdom enables us to bring the government of heaven to Earth to intervene in situations, circumstances, and relationships in which we otherwise would have no power.

The Battle that Rages Inside

To understand something is different from only knowing about something. I believe kingdom understanding is when knowledge, godly insight, and experience converge and become wisdom for us. I also believe that understanding is the purest form of power available on the earth. It is knowledge, but it is not based on intellect alone. Understanding is the ability to see what is not seen with the earth-born eye and to know what is not known by earthly intellect and reason. That may seem simple, but it is profound. Understanding is what makes up the fabric of our lives.

The mind is the seat of the intellect, and we have the capacity to develop and program our mind. This is both a responsibility and a privilege. Our education, environment, family, friends, and every other influence we are exposed to work together to form the thoughts, feelings, opinions, and emotions that flow from our mind. These thoughts may be true and excellent, or they may be false and distorted. It all depends on our programming.

Our environment has become so busy and demanding, primarily because our society has become so predominantly sense-driven. We are very dependent on and influenced by what we can taste, touch, smell, see, and hear. Our physical desires play a huge role in this; nearly everything we do is motivated by a passionate pursuit of satisfying our senses and emotional wants and needs.

That is why we make so many decisions based on what feels right. We are not always even conscious of these motives; sometimes they feel like instinct. We must remain competitive because everyone else is competitive, right? We are driven to succeed with these strategies because that is what people do, right? These kinds of drives seem right, and sometimes they are. They can also be distorted because of flawed understanding.

Our choices are clearer when we understand ourselves. Life can be frustrating, especially if we do not understand how we were created and designed to function. If we do not grasp the concepts of His kingdom, we can live our entire lives in a way that runs completely contrary to the plans of the Architect who designed us. Many of us are simply too busy to take the time to think about our reasons and our true motives. Doing what? Satisfying our senses. Gratifying our mind and body. This is not God's best for us; He has so much more in store!

In the first chapter of God's Word, we are told that we were created in the image and likeness of our Creator. I know there are plenty of people who believe otherwise—that we evolved from lower species—but I am too practical to believe that the delicate, intricate organization and profound beauty present in the universe just happened by accident. The human body alone could not be the result of chaotic collisions and random processes. Chaos never creates organization. Science itself does not allow for such a possibility. Even beyond the arguments, I can tell you from my own experience: I have personally met the Creator; He has created us in His image.

God is, always was, and will forever be the One who has provided a clear and easily understood plan for our lives. He knows how we are designed to operate, the proper function of our makeup, and how we can live in power, peace, and understanding on Earth. His plans for us are always good; He gives us constant hope. He is always offering us a future in every area. Without fail, His plans are never for disaster or frustration. He wants us to have understanding.

Why do we have such difficulty in this life? The answer is simple: we do not understand ourselves or how we are made to operate. We are made to be like our Creator—in His image (Genesis 1:27)—so we need to know His makeup and how He operates. We can understand ourselves when we realize that our design and operation parallel His.

Our Triune Nature

God's Word tells us that our Creator is one. We believe in one God, not many. But this one God functions in three distinct, definable forms—three persons united in one being. That may seem complicated, and many have made it more complex with difficult explanations. Our finite mind is not going to fully grasp an infinite God, but we can understand that this is who He says He is.

I like to compare the makeup of our Creator to the design and function of water. The substance we call H2O can be liquid (water), solid (ice), or vapor (steam), but its essence is still water. It comes in three different forms and operates in three different ways, but it is still the same substance. Our Creator is referred to as the Father who is God, the Son who is God, and the Holy Spirit who is God. All are distinctly different in design and function, but all are the same in substance.

We do not worship three gods, as some critics would argue. We worship one God in three Persons (or forms). Any casual but sincere reader who investigates this reality in God's Word will be able to understand it without question. Taking this a step further, if our design parallels His image, then we must also have three different forms. If so, these three respective forms would have distinct functions, which would be integrated as one substance. Understanding this provides clarity about our own makeup and operation that empowers us to be what our Creator designed us to be—individually, collectively, and corporately.

The three forms in every human being are the spirit, the soul (mind), and the body. Like our Creator, we have three forms with distinctly different functions. Just as the Holy Spirit God does not operate in the same way or perform the same function as God the Father, the human soul or mind does not operate in the same way or perform the same function as the human spirit.

Why is this important? Think about what would happen if you tried to use ice to perform the function of steam, or vice versa—like using steam to cool your tea or ice to remove layers of dirt and grime from an old engine. What if trying to use your mind to perform the function of your spirit accomplished the same futile results? It does not work. The result is complete frustration.

No one would confuse the different functions of different forms of water. They are common knowledge. Sadly, however, many people misunderstand the different forms of a human being. If you have ever wondered why it can be so frustrating to communicate with God, to discover His will, or to find direction, this is why. Just as ice will not perform as steam, the soul or mind will not do what the spirit is designed to do. If you have never learned the difference between your spirit and your mind or developed the distinct capabilities of each, you could struggle your entire life trying to make one perform the other's function.

Let's look at the three forms of our being that parallel God's makeup. If our being is like His, then it makes sense that He left directions or instructions about the purpose and development of each form.

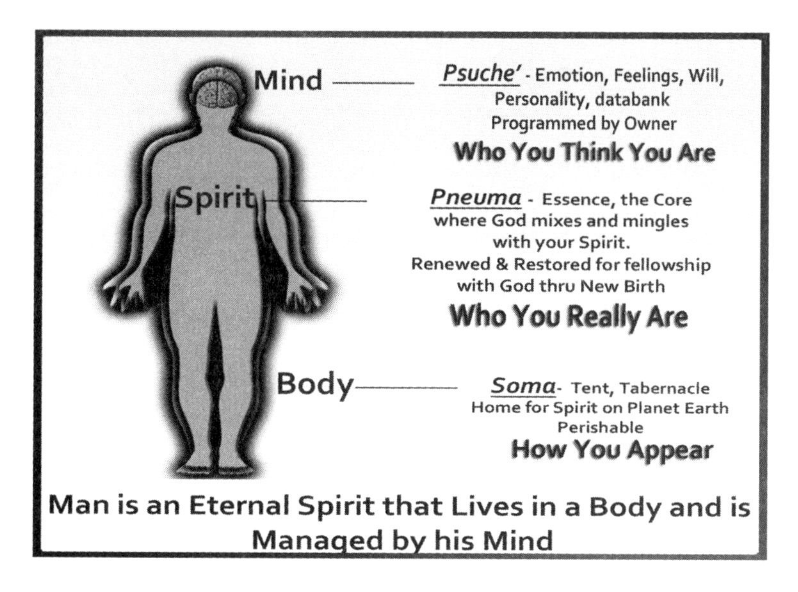

The Spirit

The Greek word most often used for "spirit" is *pneuma*. It also means "wind" or "breath." When used for human beings, it describes our essence—the core, the heart, the eternal part of us that never dies. Your spirit is eternal and functions from the vantage point of eternity. Your spirit is the real you, the core of who you are underneath all the baggage and misperceptions and emotional wounds you have accumulated over the years. Out of our spirit flow the issues of our life. We are told in God's Word to guard it and protect it, to keep it pure. It is the part of us that experiences new birth and new life, where the Holy Spirit God comes to live and empower us (John 3:5-7). This is where the kingdom of God resides. God mixes and mingles with human beings in their spirit (1 Corinthians 6:17).

Your spirit is where God comes to reside in you. It is the throne or habitation of God in your life. It is either alive in you through Jesus or dead because of sin (Romans 8:9-11; Ephesians 2:1-5). This is where light is created and darkness is destroyed. When Jesus told a woman that a person must worship God in spirit and in truth (John 4:24), He meant that worship must come from the spirit. Nothing in this world is more important than the well-being of your spirit. It is our most important form.

Because your spirit is so important, it must receive more attention and greater tending than your mind or your body. It must be the most developed part of you. God's desire is for it to be the strongest, most powerful, most dominating form of your being. It is meant to direct and instruct your mind and body. We are urged to guard and protect our spirit at all times and at all costs.

The Soul: Our Mind, Will, and Emotions

The Greek word used for "soul" is *psuche*. The literal translation is "mind." It is the root word from which we get "psychology," or the study of the mind. The mind is significant because it functions as the gatekeeper between the spirit, mind, and body. It chooses what we listen to and obey. When speaking of the soul, some theologians say it comprises the mind, will, and emotions. Basically, it is our intellect—the location of it is the location of all the learning we obtain in our educational endeavors. It is also the seat of our emotions—the place where we experience joy, happiness, fear, sadness, love, hatred, anger, bitterness, and more. It is the form that contains our personalities, our feelings, and our imaginations.

The Scriptures tell us that the mind can be tricky and deceitful. Even after the rebirth of our spirit, we must change our mind. The spirit changes immediately, but the mind requires a process of renewal (Romans 12:1-2). The mind is a database where we store information. Our mind is to be a reflection of our Creator, and He will change the way we think if we let Him.

As we grow and mature in our faith, our mind will slowly recalibrate to align with His kingdom. As we are renewed and our mind is transformed, we will increase in our ability to know and understand what we are to do in all situations. We will understand His will. God will not receive worship from or communicate with our mind. He speaks instead to our spirit and receives worship from our spirit (John 4:23-24).

The Body

The Greek word for the human body is *soma*. It is often described as a tabernacle, tent, house, or dwelling place. Our body houses our spirit on Earth. That makes the body very important because our Creator has chosen to express Himself on Earth through each person's eternal spirit that inhabits a body. It is no joke that our body is, literally, our "Earth suit." It is undeniable that our body is temporary and will die—ashes to ashes and dust to dust—but this is where our spirit lives when we are on Earth. When the spirit leaves the body, the body dies.

God's Word says that the Holy Spirit God lives in your body and that you should offer your body as a servant for that purpose (Romans 12:1). Your body is to allow the Spirit of your Creator to express Himself through your spirit in tangible, visible form. Though it is mortal (i.e., it will die), your body plays a very important role in the visible expression of God. In summation, the human spirit is an eternal spirit that lives in a body and is managed by the mind.

Empowered in Body, Mind, and Spirit

How can knowing the difference between these three forms empower us? How does it free us from frustration? We study, research, and meditate on the Scriptures, which are the agreement, the Constitution, the manual that God gave us. We do this regularly— daily, if possible. We saturate ourselves in it. The words of His Book are powerful. They are alive, separating for us what is spirit (life) and what is soul or mind (death) (Hebrews 4:12). They create knowledge in our experiences.

For example, when a thought that brings condemnation or guilt pops into your mind, you can immediately know that it is not coming from God. It is based on your emotions and feelings and is a product of your mind, which you evaluate by your spirit. Your spirit knows there is no condemnation for those who are in Christ (Romans 8:1). So, when we make mistakes, the Holy Spirit God will convict us to repent, we must ask for forgiveness, then we receive the forgiveness and new life He offers. We do not live under condemnation.

As our mind is renewed and we grow in intimacy with Christ as well as in a better understanding of our eternal identity (spirit), we are better able to control our emotions and imaginations (mind). We are more capable of recognizing the thieves of guilt and shame, to take those thoughts and emotions captive, then to bring a kingdom understanding to the situation. This allows us to more swiftly recognize, confront, and rebuke these negative emotions and imaginations when they assault us.

The by-products of our unrenewed mind produce death—and very often this destructiveness occurs in our emotions and imaginations; however, the Scriptures very often describe God in emotional terms. Emotions are a gift from Him and can be inspired by Him. Scripture is full of examples of the Holy Spirit God filling someone with emotions like compassion, joy, zeal, sorrow, and even anger.

Jesus Himself displayed the same emotions on numerous occasions. Our feelings are part of who we are as people made in God's image. They can also be exploited by our unrenewed mind, which can distort information and produce fear, anxiety, worry, bitterness, shame, and doubt.

The old saying is that we need to take captive all the fiery arrows of the world, the flesh, and the defeated Satan. Oftentimes, as we discussed in an earlier chapter, the enemy will attempt to exploit us through our mind, will, and emotions (our soul). That is why it is critical that we bring our thoughts and emotions into submission to our spirit—renewed and reprogrammed, and aligned with kingdom truth, values, and excellence.

We are meant to be believers, not doubters. We declare that we hold fast to our confession of faith. We decide to walk by faith and to practice faith, which comes by hearing the Word of God (Romans 10:17). We have a choice to follow either life or death. We choose life by receiving God's truth in our spirit and letting our spirit rule over our mind.

As newborn babies, our world centers around our body—there, we find safety, nutrition, and comfort. Those are our needs. As we grow and mature, our mind becomes more active as we perceive and absorb the world around us. Finally, we come to the age when we become attuned with our spirit. This is when we have the ability to make the decision to follow Christ or not. There is a progression here—and it is important that we recognize and affirm our spirit.

A quick look around today's world reveals that people get stuck in the first two phases of life—the body and mind—and sadly, never step into life in the spirit. Paul was disheartened by the behavior of the church at Corinth, which had been weakened by fleshly habits and desires. He alludes to the maturation process when he says:

When I was a child, I spoke about childish matters, for I

> *saw things like a child and reasoned like a child. But the day came when I matured, and I set aside my childish ways.*
> —1 Corinthians 13:11 (TPT)

Paul is literally telling the Corinthians to stop acting like children who are selfishly preoccupied with "mind and body" pursuits. It is no secret that twenty-first century America is not unlike first-century Corinth. That is why it is so important to saturate ourselves in His Word. Indeed, our exposure to our Creator's Word shows us the knowledge that comes only from Him. This is not Earth realm-born knowledge; it is beyond the natural. It involves miraculous understanding from God and operating in eternality.

Supernatural, miraculous, knowledge, wisdom, and discernment are delivered by God through our spirit and into our mind. This supernatural process then changes our thinking so that it reflects the mind of God. That is how we gain wisdom. Real wisdom is not the result of observing the situations, circumstances, and relationships around us then drawing our own conclusions about them. It is the understanding that comes from God and is not available from any other source. We receive wisdom and understanding through exposure to His Word, His prophets, His teachers, and all His ministers who are under the anointing and direction of the Holy Spirit God.

That kind of wisdom leads to understanding. We see how knowledge and wisdom fit into God's plans and purposes. When we have this wisdom and understanding, we are better equipped for the situations, circumstances, and relationships that the evil one tries to use to deceive us and cause us to doubt God. We are fully persuaded, convinced beyond doubt, and committed to the reality of His promises.

God is not changed by circumstances; He changes circumstances.

We can declare His Word fully knowing that it will not return to us without accomplishing what He said it would accomplish for those who believe. We hold fast to our confession of faith. Then we choose to walk by faith, boldly declaring that we are who He says we are, we have what He says we have, and we can and will do what He declares we can do. God's eternal kingdom will illuminate your knowledge and turn it into godly wisdom. I put it like this:

> **Knowledge** is knowing and understanding facts.
>
> **Wisdom** is knowing how to apply the knowledge to your life, personally.
>
> **Understanding** is power. Lesser authority always yields to greater authority, and there is no greater authority than our Creator God. Declare that the words of your Creator are stronger than anything that has declared itself to be superior or has exalted itself over God in your life, be it sickness, disease, drugs, alcohol, lying spirits, sexual immorality, lust, pride, all principalities and powers, every ruler of darkness, all named and unnamed spiritual wickedness in high places, every force of the kingdom of darkness.

You can rise and be healed in the name of Jesus. Pick up your bed and walk. Our Creator came to destroy all the works of the defeated Satan. He has stripped the forces of darkness of all their authority and put them under the feet of the believer. They cannot stand against the Word of God, and we will not allow them to do so.

Do not make the mistake of thinking this process of hearing from God is an emotion or a product of the mind. It is belief, the acceptance and the faith that are the product of our reborn, renewed spirit. That faith has been planted in our spirit to provide the abundant, extravagant, lavish life of liberty promised by the Word of our God. Receive it.

Shaping the Future

Proverbs 23:7 says that what we think about and meditate on directs our lives and our outcomes. This is why understanding the difference between spirit and mind is important—and why the mind must be renewed and enabled to accept God's thoughts. Vision is important; without it, "the people perish" (Proverbs 29:18 KJV). Myles Munroe points out that our thoughts become precepts, our precepts become beliefs, and beliefs become our vision and outcomes. Our thoughts are powerful.[2]

It is also very important to write our thoughts down. In Habakkuk 2:2, the prophet was told to write his vision down and make it plain. I believe recording our vision is often the flame that keeps the vision before us and leads to its ultimate fulfillment in our lives. There are plenty of examples of this in Scripture. God had a plan for an ark, and Noah had to record it. God had a plan for His people, and Moses had to record it. God had a plan for His temple, and David had to record it so Solomon could build it.

God has a plan for His kingdom government to come to Earth, and many people have recorded various aspects of that plan and sought the fulfillment of it. He also has a plan for each one of us, and we must record it for ourselves. This is one of the great benefits of keeping a journal. Many wise, godly people have encouraged the keeping of a journal.

God often speaks to people about a nation or an individual's future, and writing down His vision is a key part of seeing it develop. For several years, my family has adopted the practice of seeking our vision between Thanksgiving and January 1st for the upcoming year. We ask God about every area of our lives for the new year, record those beliefs, and use them as our guides and measurements for the results. We call it our "Family, Business, and Ministry Plan."

The late, great South Korean pastor and leader David Yonggi Cho recommended this in one of his early books: write down even the smallest details of what we are asking and believing. It has always been our experience that God will do great things if we listen with our spirit to what He says, write down what we hear, share it with each other, and agree together for their accomplishment.

God has not always fulfilled the visions Fran and I receive—sometimes He far exceeds them. We expect Him to do so. He instructs us in His Word to stay busy and plant a variety of crops because you never know which ones will grow. Maybe they all will. Whatever we see with the eyes of our spirit allows us to be believers and not doubters. The vision we paint on the canvas in our mind is our faith we present to the Holy Spirit God to fulfill.

Our thoughts and imagination can be images of faith or of doubt. When we doubt, not only is that unbelief in what is true; it is also belief in what is not true. We create an alternate imagination in our mind that we have faith in. Doubt is just another form of faith, although it is faith in the wrong image. That imagery can become a huge stumbling block. We are told to bring every thought and imagination, everything that exalts itself against the knowledge of God, into captivity to Christ (2 Corinthians 10:5).

The reason this is difficult for many people is that they do not have the right understanding of God, His Word, or coming into agreement.

This happens when an individual's spirit has not received His Word to the degree that it has transformed their mind. That can only come in relationship with Him—not just from being born again, but from being in an active, in-depth relationship with Him. Such a person has been redeemed but has not necessarily been restored.

During a particularly frustrating time in my life when I was still struggling with kingdom understanding, I asked God, "Lord, does Your Word work or not?" That is when He told me I needed to understand the good news of restoration. Jesus told Nicodemus that we have to be born again, but that is only the beginning. Faith is not just for getting into the kingdom; it is also for what we do when we get there.

I lived as a defeated Christian for many years because I did not understand the difference between redemption and restoration. God's Word was not the problem. I needed to understand that God has been and is restoring us back to original glory, just as if we have never sinned. How else are we going to live in power and authority in this world? It is not simply by being redeemed, but by being restored and embracing our reestablished original glory. There is much taught about original sin, but practically nothing about original glory.

If we do not understand what restoration is, we will not get there. We must believe and understand that there is a restoration process. Restoration is when we develop the kind of relationship with God that Adam and Eve had in the Garden before they transgressed. It is going back to where we were before; it is going back to original glory. But it's important to understand that the new birth creates a citizen of the kingdom; it does not create a restored person. Restoration can only come through a developed relationship with the Father.

Unfortunately, most of our methods for knowing God and living in His will deal with the mind, not with the spirit. As we have seen, that is the wrong order. Our restoration process leads us in the way of the kingdom. We must receive His wisdom in our spirit, which leads to understanding, which then enables us to have unwavering faith that can shape the future.

When a thought comes to mind, we must have ourselves so programmed with the Word that we can tell the difference between our soul (mind) and our spirit to know where that thought came from. The thought must line up with the Word of God. If a thought instructs us to speak or act negatively about another, you can know that it is of our mind and our emotions, and not of our spirit. The same is true when a thought entices you to lust or take steps toward having an affair or when an idea contradicts one of God's promises. The Word of God speaks to these things, and we know anything contrary to His Word is not from Him.

Refuse to accept thoughts from the defeated Satan. Declare the words of God and walk in His ways. Let your mind be renewed according to the truth your spirit has received. As a redeemed and restored person, let faith be planted in your spirit to lead you into the abundance and blessings promised by God.

YOUR DECLARATIONS

RENEW YOUR MIND

We need to know not only the benefits of being "in Him" and of the law of the spirit of life in Christ but also the identity and attributes God gives us. It would be impossible to discover and list all of what He says and thinks about us, but the Scriptures give us many powerful statements about who we are and what we have been given. Remind yourself of these truths, let them fully sink into your heart, and say them out loud:

Prayer of Commitment to the Word

Father, in the name of Jesus, the (your name here) family, all of our heirs and all of our descendants forever, we declare that We commit ourselves to walk in Your Word. We recognize that Your Word is integrity itself; Your Word is steadfast; Your Word is sure; Your Word is eternal, and we trust our lives to the provisions of Your Word.

You have sent Your Word forth into our spirit and into our mind. We let Your Word dwell in us richly in all wisdom. Your Word does not depart out of our mouth. Your Word is all that we speak. We meditate in Your Word, day and night so that we may diligently act upon Your Word. Your Word is the incorruptible seed that is abiding and living in our spirit and in our mind. Your

Word is growing mightily in us, now. Your Word is becoming dominant and producing Your nature and Your life in me.

We thank You, Father, that Your Word is our Counsel. Your Word gives us insight and direction. Your Word is our shield. Your Word forms a hedge of protection around us that the defeated Satan cannot penetrate. Your Word is our buckler. Your Word keeps us upright and connected to You. You are our complete source and our complete supply. Your Word is our powerful weapon in battle that always gives us victory. Your Word is the lamp unto our feet and the light unto our path. Your Word makes our way straight before us, and we never stumble or fall because our steps are ordered by Your Word. We recognize the strategies and the deceits of the defeated Satan, and we put a stop to them by speaking Your Word out of our mouth in faith.

We are confident, Father, that You and Your perfect plan for our lives are at work in us, to lead us to want to do—and then to do—Your good pleasure. We exalt Your Word. We hold Your Word in the highest esteem. We give Your Word first place in our lives. We boldly and confidently declare that our spirit and mind are fixed upon You and established on the solid foundation of the living Word of God.

All of the declarations found here, and many more, are available in the book Kingdom Activating Declarations by Charlie Lewis.

Visit www.ksam.net for this and other great resources.

CHAPTER 6

THE POSITION AND IDENTITY OF A KINGDOM CITIZEN

The Piper Cub is a basic, affordable, user-friendly airplane that was great for flight training when it was being produced in the late 1930s and early 1940s. It became very popular for not only its versatility and reliability but also its simplicity. The Cub does not require a lot of training to be mastered, and many are still in use today.

The Lockheed Martin F-35 Lightning II, on the other hand, is a high-tech fighter plane with stealth, intelligence, and combat capabilities. It is highly maneuverable but difficult to master. A pilot needs intensive training and sharp skills to handle this plane's abilities. It is a powerful aircraft that can effectively and efficiently perform a wide range of functions, and it can win decisive victories over the enemy. It cannot be mastered casually.

When we are born again, we are presented with the spiritual equivalent of an F-35. We are equipped with blistering firepower and access to superior intelligence. We can devastate the enemy if we know how to use the gifts and abilities we have been given. Most people find it easier to take the Cub and do whatever they can with it. The Cub is useful and easy to operate in its place.

As far as most people know, there are no better options. Very few realize that they have been given the equivalent of a piece of precision machinery that can swing the battle dramatically in their favor. It truly is like the analogy of the British prisoners of war we examined earlier: to act like a soldier (rather than an enslaved person), one must believe they are a soldier. In this sense, being imprisoned is a mindset. It is like settling for a humble Cub aircraft when the F-35 is at one's disposal.

We have seen that the purpose of redemption is to lead us to restoration. God never intended for us to be born again yet remain uninformed, uneducated, and unequipped. Scripture says that all the power and witness of heaven is in Jesus, and we are in Him. We need to understand this transformative truth and function from its vantage point. We are in Jesus, and He is over all His enemies and everything else in this universe.

In Chapter Five, we discussed the difference between the spirit, mind, and body. We learned how the mind can be brought into alignment with the truth that God has put into our spirit through His Word, His teachers, and His prophets. Though the spirit is immediately born again and renewed, the mind must be renewed through a process of restoration or programming.

The goal of this renewal is for our inward confession—our faith and beliefs—to be thoroughly saturated in God's Word. As we reach a saturation level—receive all that He says about us and has promised to us—we are able to produce abundant fruit for His kingdom. Out of those beliefs and our agreement with His truth, we shape the future and determine the outcomes in our lives.

One of the truths we need to fully grasp is who we are in Christ. God has already put this into every believer's spirit, but our mind needs to align with this truth so we can live from this reality. We need to understand our position, fully knowing that we are in Christ and above the enemy.

To Be "In Christ"

The phrase "in Christ" or "in Him" is used repeatedly throughout the New Testament. Watchman Nee said that the two most powerful words on the earth are "in Him." There is no condemnation for those who are "in Christ" (Romans 8:1), we are seated with Christ in heavenly places (Ephesians 2:6), and we are "saints" who have been blessed "in Christ" with every spiritual blessing (Ephesians 1:1,3). We reside in His kingdom and find our identity in Him. We died with Jesus when He died on the cross, and we are raised with Him in His resurrection. It is His life that is functioning within us, in our spirit. Jesus really is our life.

This means that the responsibility for fulfillment is not a matter of what we can earn through our own efforts or through our own mind. We read His Word and believe that, in Him, we have those things He says and promises. We do not have to work up to these. From the very first day we enter the kingdom of God, we have the ability to live a restored life if we have the knowledge and understanding of what that is.

Fran and I learned this in somewhat dramatic fashion early in our marriage. As I mentioned earlier, God called us to leave the military and go help my dad run the family business in Jacksonville. Several years into that season—when we were really firing on all cylinders—God again asked us to pull up stakes and move. This time, it was across state lines to southwestern Georgia, to the town of Thomasville.

Fran was seven months pregnant, and it seemed like the worst time to move, but God had been clear that this is what He wanted from us. He put us in touch with a lovely woman named Mrs. Jordan. (She quickly corrected my pronunciation of "Jordan" and said, "That's pronounced 'Jeer-dan' here.") Her husband had passed away, and the managers of the furniture business were of retirement age. She was looking to sell. I met with her CPA, attorney, and accountant after evaluating the business and praying about a purchase price. I felt confident that the Lord had given me a price to pay, but when I presented my offer to her accountant, he said, "Mr. Lewis, she's already been offered more than that."

And I said, "Well, that's okay. Please, just give her the offer because it does not matter what she has been offered. If God wants me to have this business and this is the price he told me, then she will accept the offer."

Within twenty-four hours, he called and said, "Well, we're all shocked, but she's going to take your offer." He proceeded to introduce me to a local banker, and much to our amazement, we were immediately approved for a business loan.

We sold our lovely home in Jacksonville and moved to a town where the only soul we knew was Mrs. Jordan. It was a clear example of what happens when we take God at His Word. He was the one who threw open the doors for us—our job was to simply move forward when He did.

Faith is the currency of this kingdom. Faith is what we engage to acquire the promises of our God. We are in Him as soon as we are born of His Spirit. His blood flows through our reborn veins. We are royalty. We are His co-heirs to kingdom riches. Being in Christ means that every resource that He has is at our disposal now—that all of the power and all the authority He possesses is also ours because of our relationship in Him. He has made all the necessary provision for that, and we are supposed to partake of that provision because we are in Him.

The Passion translation of Hebrews 12:23 says, "… all our names have been legally registered as citizens of heaven!" This means we have access to all that is in heaven. Indeed, the Scriptures tell us "we will have a home in heaven, an eternal body made for us by God himself and not by human hands" (2 Corinthians 5:1). We are told that "He will wipe every tear from their eyes, and there will be no more death or sorrow or crying or pain. All these things are gone forever" (Revelation 21:4). While we do not have the time to explore all of the multitude of riches mentioned in the Word about heaven, I encourage you to explore them on your own.

As well, consider these verses, which are only a small sampling of what the Word says about our "being in" Christ:

- We are a new creation (a new creature altogether) (2 Corinthians 5:17, AMPC)
- We have been made alive with Him (Colossians 2:13)
- In Christ lives all the fullness of God in a human body (Colossians 2:9-10)
- We are heirs with Christ, inheriting what He inherits as God's children (Romans 8:15)
- He is the life that lives inside of us (Galatians 2:20)
- The law of life in Christ has set us free from the law of sin and death (Romans 8:2)

As mentioned earlier, Watchman Nee said the two most powerful words in the Scriptures are "in Him." These words refer to our King and to our relationship and our position in Him. This is a position of authority, where we rest in His power and not ours. We rely on His power and ability to conquer all His enemies, to provide us with wisdom, and to guide our thoughts and steps. We throw all our concerns about fulfillment onto His shoulders.

There is no enemy equal to Him. He has declared emphatically that He will not leave us or forsake us. He has offered us all of Himself in everything we encounter. We are strengthened knowing that "the Spirit who lives in us is greater than the spirit who lives in the world" (1 John 4:4).

So why do we still struggle from a powerless position with the situations, circumstances, and relationships we find ourselves dealing with every day? Remember that the defeated Satan has no power over us. He must deceive us and get us to believe his lies. His tactics have not changed since Eden. He has been stripped of authority, but he does know how to deceive. Satan always appeals to our mind and our thoughts and our imaginations. If we struggle and seem to have no power to overcome, it is because we are not living in the reality of kingdom understanding of the truth.

If we consider anything in Scripture from any perspective other than a kingdom understanding, it can lead to confusion and wrong assumptions. To be overcomers and to realize victory in our situations, circumstances, and relationships, we need to understand the law of the spirit of life in Christ, which sets us free from the law of sin and death (Romans 8:2). This makes our position in Christ not just a truth we know about but the reality we experience.

The New Testament Dynamic

In our study of the systems of God's kingdom government, we see many principles and dynamics that function on an *if-then* basis. We call them the dynamics of conduct and behavior, which have sure and certain outcomes. We make a choice, then we experience the results and consequences of that choice. If we confess and believe God's Word no matter what the situation, circumstance, or relationship we find around us, we can receive what He has said and promised.

How do we approach dynamics as people who are positioned in Christ, who has set us free from the law? In the New Testament, the "law of the spirit of life in Christ Jesus" appears to be the only place where the word "law" is used. It is not referring to a body of written instructions like the law of Moses or the law of the prophets. Those are *if-then* dynamics. The law of the spirit of life in Christ is better seen as a *then-do* dynamic. It is an already completed, settled, established fact. We function out of what has already been accomplished. We must forgive to be forgiven.

Compare this to a law of nature like gravity. Gravity is there, and we do not have to do anything to make it work. Gravity is the product of design. It is a principle God established for the earth. It is not Scripture; it is operational. If we recognize the principle and the design of gravity and respect, follow, and obey it, it will work for us and for our good. If we do not follow the principles, thinking perhaps we can drive off a cliff or jump off a building without experiencing the consequences, the results can be devastating and tragic. It will work regardless of what we do, whether we honor it or not, but our attitude toward it and our response to it determines whether it works for us or against us.

The law of the spirit of life in Christ has made us free from the law of sin and death, and therefore we are not subject to the defeated Satan (Romans 8:2). It is an established fact, just as sure and real as the dynamic of gravity. We receive the benefit if we recognize and honor the dynamical principle. God's Angel Armies are assigned to assist believers and perform the Word of God in our lives if we will recognize and engage those words by calling them into our need (Hebrews 1:14).

The challenge seems to be our inability to recognize and honor the completed work of Christ. If we do not know and we do not understand this law as a dynamic of design, we cannot apply this reality to our daily lives. Whether we recognize the completed work of this law or not, it is there and it is working. Our failure to recognize and honor it can bring tragic and often devastating results to our walk.

We can correct this and walk in the active authority of this dynamic reality. Nineteen times in Romans, we are told by the Holy Spirit God to "reckon" or to "consider" the law of sin and death to be destroyed in our lives (Romans 6:11, for one example). We are to think and act on the true assumption that this law and the defeated Satan have no power and influence over us anymore. That does not mean it is gone, annihilated, wiped off the face of the earth, or nonexistent. It is repeatedly clear in Scripture that this power and influence are defeated.

Most, if not all, believers are approached repeatedly, day after day after day, by the forces of evil from the kingdom of darkness. Those forces want us to accept the dialogue of gloom, doom, and despair as well as the thoughts they bombard us with. They provoke thoughts and ideas that agree with the law of sin and death and the defeated Satan. Has our King, the true and the living God, left us helpless and hopeless? Of course not. That is not even a reasonable suggestion.

No, God tells us to "reckon" the influence of those thoughts to be destroyed in our lives and to bring anything that is contrary to the words of the King into captivity to what He has said and is saying. He is alive, and He speaks the truth of His kingdom governance to us clearly. God is Spirit, and His Spirit mixes and mingles with our spirit.

By His Word, He speaks to our spirit and makes the way clear. We must recognize the strategies and deceits of the defeated Satan, and we must put a stop to them by speaking His Word out loud in faith, just as Jesus did when tempted by Satan. Jesus' reply was always, "It is written." We believe in our spirit and confess with our mouth to bring salvation—the answer.

A Two-Part Victory Plan

This is our two-part victory plan: believe and confess. In numerous verses in Romans, we are told to "reckon" or "consider" (depending on the translation) certain truths about our position in Christ and the reality of the law of the spirit of life in Christ and the law of sin and death. This word is *logidzomai* in Greek, and it has a double meaning. It is a legal or courtroom term, as well as an accounting or bookkeeping term. In the courtroom, it has the legal ramifications of something that has already been determined.

It is an established law, and we do not have to do anything to make it active; however, we must recognize, understand, and apply its disciplines and principles to our situations, circumstances, and relationships—and, more importantly, to our thoughts. Failure to do so does not mean the law or condition is not there or that it is not working. It simply means we are not engaging the benefits of the law of the spirit of life in Christ in our lives. That can be devastating and produce tragic results.

As with an accounting word, it is like entering a transaction into a checkbook. We are to count this law of the spirit of life as being in our account—included in each situation, circumstance, relationship, and thought—that is it part of our available balance. It has been deposited in our account and is available for us to spend. We must not only write the check, but we must also cash the check. Furthermore, this is an asset that can never be depleted. It is an unlimited supply and is being renewed constantly. It is more than we can ask or imagine, and our account can never be overdrawn.

Because this supply is more than we can think or imagine, we need to become really good at thinking and imagining. We are instructed not to think as the world (the kingdom of darkness) thinks but to allow our King to change the way we think. Our thoughts are to become like His. We are to reprogram our mind so our thoughts agree with His Word, His ability, and His provision.

Can our victory plan really be that simple? In the kingdom, it is. Everything God created works in a system. The heavens, our bodies, the environment of Earth—these and everything else He made function by the laws and dynamics He put into place. Under the law of the spirit of life in Christ, we must believe what His Word says in our spirit, declare it to be so with our mouth, and follow the disciplines He has provided. Then, what He has declared will be our reality.

This means we must "reckon" our freedom and fight against the influence of the law of sin and death and the defeated Satan. We must choose the armor of God and wield it against feelings of powerlessness and the attacks and aggravations of the enemy. On the other hand, we must "reckon" ourselves to be alive to Christ under the law of the spirit of life. This legally binding, accounting-sheet transaction allows us to tread upon serpents and scorpions and all the power of the defeated enemy (Luke 10:19).

We take our shield of faith, and we quench every fiery dart of the vanquished and defeated Satan (Ephesians 6:16). The enemy is under our feet; we can crush his head with our heel. Greater is He who is living in and working through us than he who is in this world (1 John 4:4). In every situation, we are made to triumph in Christ (2 Corinthians 2:14). It is "in Him" that we live and move and have our being (Acts 17:28).

YOUR DECLARATIONS

KNOW WHO YOU ARE

You will want to pray the truth of your position and identity in Christ, daily. You will need to personalize it for yourself:

Father, in the name of Jesus (say your name and the names of your family members here), and all of our heirs and all of our descendants forever, we declare our allegiance to You. You are the true and living God. You are the only wise God, our Father. There is no other God. You are our complete source and our complete supply. We will never look to anyone or to anything else for our provision. You give us power, and You give us strength to be successful so that You may establish Your covenant with us. We are victors.

We walk in victory over all the forces of the kingdom of darkness through our faith in You, Jesus. You are the Son of God, and You are God Himself. You made each of us unique and special and like no one else. You have given us a unique purpose that is good and full of hope. You recreated us in Your image and in Your likeness.

You have forgiven us and birthed us anew through Your own blood and through our faith in You. Our old life is gone. We are, now, a new creation through Your workmanship. We can and we do all things through You. You have assigned, and you have charged, the Angel Armies of God to keep us safe on land, in the air, and on the sea. In every situation, in each circumstance, and in all of our relationships, the Angel Armies of God prevent us from being harmed, injured, and from stumbling.

You have chosen us and made us Your friends and Your family. You love us with an everlasting, unfailing love. You have made us important in Your kingdom as Your chosen people. We rule on the earth as Royal Priests in Your courts. We are the apple of Your eye and Your very own treasured possession. We will live to declare Your Glory and display Your Power and Your Praises on Earth as they are in Heaven.

May Your kingdom come; may Your will be done in all of Your Creation on earth as it is in heaven. In Jesus' name we pray, amen.

All of the declarations found here, and many more, are available in the book Kingdom Activating Declarations by Charlie Lewis.

Visit www.ksam.net for this and other great resources.

CHAPTER 7

THE BELIEFS AND FAITH OF A KINGDOM CITIZEN

Our move to Thomasville, Georgia was difficult at first but soon became a fruitful time for Fran and me. Little did we know that we would remain there. More than four decades later, we still call it home. When we first moved, of course, we had no idea what God was going to do with a pair of transplanted Floridians now living in a relatively small town in rural Georgia. Our oldest son, Zach, was born just two months after we moved out of our small Thomasville apartment and into our first home.

Over the next few years, the Lord opened incredible doors for us, and the furniture business was a great success. Our family was thriving as well, as our second son, Nick, was born just over two years after Zach.

I was experiencing a season of seemingly unquenchable thirst for God's Word and fellowship with Him, and as a result, I was spending more time than usual with Him and His Spirit. During one of these study times, the Lord asked me to do something that shocked me. Well, He did not "ask" as much as He told me. And it was not so much *what* He was telling me to do but the manner of *how* He was telling me to do it.

The Lord said, "I want you to close the furniture store. I want you to have a 'Going Out of Business' sale."

It was that specific—and I was not at all happy. If I was not happy, Fran was even less so. Livid would probably be more accurate. You must understand that we had already made two "Abraham and Sarah" moves: one from military life, and the second when we left Jacksonville, leaving behind all our friends and our amazing youth group. We had started very small in Thomasville and worked hard to make our furniture business successful. It was now thriving. Not only that, but we were both very active in the local business community.

I tried to barter with God. Things were thriving, and it was the perfect time to sell. "How about if we just sell it quietly, Lord, without telling a lot of people?" He said, clearly, no. He wanted us to have the Going out of Business sale (GOB sale). I reasoned with the Holy Spirit—or argued with Him, actually—for several weeks. The Spirit would not agree.

I will let Fran tell her side of the story:

> I (Fran) was not at all happy when Charlie shared what the Lord had instructed him about a "going out of business" sale. That is what businesses do when they are struggling or trying to avoid bankruptcy. Yet, that was the exact opposite of what was happening with our business.
>
> A GOB sale has a certain stigma associated with it, and I did not want us to experience that. We had worked very hard at building the business and at establishing respect in our business community and relationships. It was embarrassing to have a GOB sale, especially since

the business was successful and thriving. Our accounts receivables were more than they had ever been, and we were collecting a higher monthly percentage than ever before. Our sales had tripled; our inventory was at an all-time high; everything was mostly paid for, and our property had recently been completely refurbished.

I was upset and asked God, "Why do You want us to do it this way? This looks like we are a failure. This business is doing well and better than it ever has. This could ruin our reputation in town." I had a laundry list of things I was fighting with God about.

Then one day, I was getting ready to take Zach to kindergarten—a hectic morning trying to get out the door. I was particularly angry as I was set to leave the house with Zach and baby Nick. At that moment, I reached out to grab the doorknob to yank the door open and make my way down the driveway and into the car. But, as I put my hand on the doorknob, the Holy Spirit spoke to me. I mean, it was just like you and me talking to each other. He said, "Fran," and got my attention.

I stopped short and responded, "Yes, Lord?"

He said, "In a very short time, not too far down the road, you are going to see that what you are calling evil and bad today is going to be one of the best things that has ever happened to you. Just trust Me!"

He sovereignly spoke that to me, and I was taken aback. It was so direct. I had to say, "Yes, Lord; yes Lord." It was a defining moment—not just for that business decision, but for our future. And it was not

> like I suddenly liked the idea of a GOB sale. I still did not like the directive, but I knew that it was exactly what we had to do.

After much prayer and soul-searching, Fran and I agreed to the plan. I did say, however, "Okay, God. If it is a GOB sale You want, then I am willing to do that. I am asking you for three things: One, I want someone to buy our accounts, and I am asking you for eighty-five cents on the dollar. Two, I want the person who buys our inventory to have access to a significant amount of additional inventory and for them to also include that inventory in the sale. Three, I want to run the sale myself and make significant money in the process."

Having been in the furniture business most of my life, I knew any one of those requests was a huge challenge if not impossible. They would be very difficult to accomplish through a GOB sale and impossible without divine intervention. I was not consciously trying to block God's request, but I am not sure if that is not what was going on subconsciously.

To my shock, within two weeks all three requests were met, without much effort on my part. It was an amazing experience, and the yield was more than we had made the entire time we had operated the business.

Some people believed it was a defeat for our business to have a GOB sale. I have found that often when we hear and follow the Spirit, people influenced by the kingdom of darkness see it as a failure by their standards, and they are not bashful about sharing their opinions.

Fran says, "God was obviously testing our level of obedience, and as I look back on my 'doorknob moment,' I can honestly say that He was checking my heart, seeing if I was willing to fully surrender our 'reputation' and the world's definition of 'success,' which varies so radically from God's definition. That was an opportunity for Charlie and me to choose obedience and integrity with God over the opinions and gossip of the community around us."

I wholeheartedly agree with Fran. And yes, while there have certainly been times in my life when I failed God or did not listen to His "still, small voice," in this case, I am very thankful that I did. I believe that He was putting us through His school of redemptive kingdom understanding—giving us a glimpse of how His kingdom operates on Earth. Oftentimes, what the world sees as foolishness, God sees as wisdom. The economics of His system do not mimic those of the world's fallen system. I call this divine system "kingdomnomics." As I mentioned in the Introduction, it is the title and subject of the second book in this trilogy. Kingdomnomics are radically different from the way conventional earthly wisdom operates. As good as the furniture business was, it could not provide for all that our God had planned for us. We waited for almost a year, asking for direction for the next step. Fran was not comfortable with the waiting, but I knew in my spirit, we were following and obeying God. Amazingly, after just over a year of waiting and praying, within a two-week period, God miraculously opened doors and facilitated the connections for the insurance business and the jewelry business. Both of which have been tremendously more lucrative than the furniture business. And both without any financial investment outlay from us. As my friend Jerry Anderson likes to say, "only God."

It takes a major paradigm shift to move from the world's false kingdom system into God's kingdom reality. For those of us who were not raised with an understanding of His "on earth as it is in heaven" kingdom, it can be a "from the ground up" process. It is sometimes easier to build a home from scratch than it is to refurbish an older home. And so it was with us: Fran and I had to unlearn a lot of religious thinking for God to restore us so we could understand His real kingdom. As we pursue Him and study His Word, He is faithful and true to speak to us and to teach us His kingdom ways. Jesus said Himself,

> *My own sheep will hear my voice and I know each one, and they will follow me. I give to them the gift of eternal life and they will never be lost and no one has the power to snatch them out of my hands. My Father, who has given them to me as his gift, is the mightiest of all, and on one has the power to snatch them from my Father's care.*
>
> —John 10:27–29 (TPT)

We do not worship a pagan god of stone or seek the mystical mumblings of an archaic oracle. Rather, we are part of our Shepherd's sheepfold—the place of safety (like a corral) where Jesus tends to us. There are the wild places (the world), and then there is the sheepfold, where He covers us as a mother hen who gathers her chicks. We are not wandering aimlessly and hoping to stumble into truth. And when we do stray, He tells us that He will leave the ninety-nine to find the one (Matthew 18:12). How amazing is it that this God we worship is a benevolent, loving, forgiving King!

Understanding the Roots of Our Faith

As we have discussed, embracing His kingdom is more than finding salvation and being redeemed. It is a process of wisdom and knowledge that the Shepherd desires to give to us. Like excavating a beautiful ancient building, we must understand the roots of the foundations of our faith. We must gain knowledge of the riches to be unearthed when we gain kingdom citizenship.

That is why understanding the source of our beliefs is very important. You may ask, "But how do we discover what we do not know?" We go back to the beginning. We pursue His truth through His Word to appropriate the roots, shoots, and fruits of our faith.

Most of us grew up simply absorbing our beliefs, as if by osmosis, from our surroundings—our family, friends, church, education, government, media, entertainment, and more. Many people do this and never even consider whether the messages they are receiving and their basic assumptions are correct. We may not trust every one of these sources, but we trust enough of them, especially parents and close friends, to accept their messages without question.

These influences are best described as culture. Culture can be defined as the customary beliefs, social forms, and material traits of a racial, religious, or social group. It is defined by the shared attitudes, values, goals, and practices that characterize that group. Most of what we learn from our culture is not intentional. Much is absorbed. We pick it up naturally from living in our surroundings.

The difficulty with this approach to our beliefs is that it is not stable. Like a poorly made spinning top, it wobbles and moves unpredictably. Even in our own lifetime, we can observe that the attitudes, values, goals, and practices of our nation and our world have changed, often dramatically. Our beliefs must be established in a culture that is based on absolute truth—that does not change—according to the redemptive Kingdom System we have been provided.

If we were to single out one stark difference—of the hundreds we could choose from—between scriptural truth and the world's notion of truth, this would be it: we live in a post-Christian age where God's Word is not seen by most people as fully dependable, accurate, or relevant. Cultural, false kingdom, "truth" is malleable, adjustable, and individually customizable. For that reason alone, kingdom believers will be persecuted for believing in absolute truth. Jesus is clear about this.

That is why it is difficult for many to walk through His narrow gate. It is the reason that the rich young ruler in Mark 10 walked away sad. Jesus asked Him to give up all his wealth and follow Jesus, but the young man was unable to do it. It is what prompted Jesus to say to His disciples,

> *"Jesus looked at the faces of his disciples and said, 'How hard it is for the wealthy to enter into God's kingdom realm." The disciples were startled when they heard this. But Jesus again said to them, 'Children, it is next to impossible for those who trust in their riches to find their way into God's kingdom. It is easier to stuff a rope through the eye of a needle than for a wealthy person to enter into God's kingdom.'"*
>
> —Mark 10:23–25 (TPT)

While Jesus was responding specifically to this wealthy young man's inability to give up His earthly possessions to gain God's greater ones, the principle applies to anything we covet or idolize. We do not need to be wealthy to struggle with choosing His narrow path. Just as a financially rich person can indeed enter the kingdom of God, a person of lower socioeconomic status may choose the earth's pleasures over God's kingdom. Satan tests and tempts all of us with those shiny but worldly things that most appeal to our flesh. For one person it is money, while for another it might be power, control, alcohol, sex, or any myriad of other things.

Basically, our modern world—especially in western nations—has bought into the lie that we can curate and customize our own version of the truth. Essentially, this would mean that each can be his or her own god. Does that sound outrageous? Consider what the serpent did to Eve when he lied and said, "God knows that if you eat of the forbidden tree, you will be like him," then remember that God's kingdom is not an oligarchy or a democracy. He rules supreme; only He is omniscient.

Just as with the Ekklesia at Corinth, the deceptions and warped lies of the enemy have seeped into today's church. I am not here to bash or judge; however, we must filter everything we hear and learn through the only truly pure filtration system, His Word, as led and fed by His Holy Spirit.

Over the past fifty years, the bottled water industry has grown exponentially. Think about it: everywhere we go people drink healthy water. Whether it is spring water, distilled water, purified water (by osmosis or any of several other filtering processes), or water imported from pure spring sources as far away as Fiji or Iceland. There are now even water bars where you can sample H20 from around the globe.

In the 1970s, just 350 million gallons of bottled water were being sold in the United States—about a gallon and a half per person per year.[3] With the help of the French water company Perrier, which undertook an ambitious marketing strategy in the late 1970s, water bottle sales in the US began to rise and have not stopped rising for almost fifty years.

In 2022, 15.9 billion gallons of bottled water were sold in the United States. Over the last ten years, the country's bottled water sales volume has increased considerably with each consecutive year.[4]

Even the most casual observer can look around and see our nation's passion for pure water. Ironically, however, in that same fifty-year period, the number of people who attend church each week has plummeted.

After World War II, churches and schools greatly expanded to accommodate the growing population, and by the 1950s, organized religion was in its heyday. On a typical Sunday morning in the period from 1955-1958, almost half of all Americans were attending church—the highest percentage in US history. From 2020 to the present, the average has been 30 percent. Recent church attendance levels are about ten percentage points lower than what Gallup measured in 2012 and most prior years.[5]

Statistics, of course, are only part of the picture. And for the most part, they can be rather depressing. But they are also an indicator of the spiritual state we are in as a culture. For those of us who are pursuing God's kingdom, it is a motivator for us to pray. It is also indicative of our culture's departure from spiritual truth into relativism.

Can you imagine informing avid bottled water drinkers that the water companies have lied to them about the purity of their water? What do you think would happen? Chaos and bedlam would ensue, class action lawsuits would be filed, and people would be up in arms. But think about the spiritual toxins and impurities the enemy has been feeding into our nation's "spiritual water system." Like Paul's message to the Corinthians, we, too, need to understand that …

> *But even if our Gospel (the glad tidings) also be hidden (obscured and covered up with a veil that hinders the knowledge of God), it is hidden [only] to those who are perishing and obscured [only] to those who are spiritually dying and veiled [only] to those who are lost. For the god of this world has blinded the unbelievers' minds [that they should not discern the truth], preventing them from seeing the illuminating light of the Gospel of the glory of Christ (the Messiah), Who is the Image and Likeness of God.*
>
> —2 Corinthians 4:3-4, AMPC

We do not need to drink the tainted water of the false kingdom. And we must understand that the purity of God's Word is stable, consistent, and everlasting. As well, His truth does not change with situations and circumstances. It is not situational. As citizens of the kingdom of God, we must not be swayed by the kingdom of darkness or by what we see around us.

The government and culture of God's kingdom does not change. This kingdom is the only entity on Earth where we will always find a stable government and constant culture. The values, dynamics, moral standards, ideals, norms, goals, and true spiritual authority of this kingdom are unchanging and 100% "certified pure" by the Creator.

Human beings long for this kingdom, and we have been charged to deliver it—the culture of heaven—to Earth. We are called to show this kingdom to those who dwell here. God's Word tells how important this is for humanity. Romans 8:19 says that all of creation is waiting for God's children to be revealed. We are not supposed to shut ourselves away from the world and await Jesus's return. Instead, we are to go into the world and preach the gospel to every tongue, tribe, and nation. Preach, in this instance, means both telling people about Jesus, and helping them find restoration into His kingdom mindset.

What are we telling the world around us? Are we showing His praises until He comes? Are we living a life of victory that is noticeably different from those around us? Does the world see the government of our God demonstrated in our lives both in our community and in our culture? Are we the ones being told and shown what values and norms and beliefs to accept?

All of humanity is looking and longing for the kingdom that has been given to us and placed inside of us. God has called us to be the birthers of His governance. Everywhere we go, we must share the good news of the Gospel of the kingdom of our God.

As we mentioned earlier, one word that is tainted with negativity in our western culture is "totalitarian." This is because it is often associated with destructive dictators and regimes led by such despots as Hitler, Stalin, and Idi Amin. This negative association, however, is because the world's false Kingdom System is always seeking God's eternal kingdom and always provides a phony substitute. Redemption is the key. Jesus told Nicodemus that you cannot see or understand His kingdom without being born again and redeemed. As His creation, in our mind and spirit, we have a God-shaped hole that can be filled only by Him. The defeated Satan twists our desire for a benevolent savior and turns men's hearts not toward God but toward counterfeits of His rule and reign in the form of despotic earthly rulers.

- The Israelites cried out for a king and they received Saul, a corrupt king who did not follow God's kingdom designs.
- The Germans cried out for clear and strong leadership after the ruin and humiliation of World War I, and instead of turning to Christ and His kingdom, they gave absolute power to Adolf Hitler.
- Out of the ashes of the Russian revolution rose the Soviet Union, a godless empire that elevated Josef Stalin and other totalitarian leaders, with devastating results.

We need to redeem the word "totalitarian" when it comes to God's heavenly kingdom for humanity, for it is indeed a redemptive totalitarian system—but one based on His indescribable and perfect love rather than the defeated Satan's human counterfeits. God's totalitarian system is grace-driven, eternal, completely redemptive, and for all mankind. The redemptive all-inclusive, totalitarian Kingdom System is made for man, and man is made for the totalitarian Kingdom System. Nothing else will fit and nothing else will work.

The Source of a Belief

Myles Munroe, a master teacher of kingdom truth, makes some profound observations about where beliefs come from and tracks how they evolve from a thought. He lists the following:

1. Original thought is a precept.
2. A conceived precept is an idea.
3. A conceived idea is a concept.
4. An accepted concept becomes a conviction.
5. An accepted conviction becomes a belief.
6. An accepted belief becomes an ideology.
7. An accepted ideology becomes a philosophy.
8. An accepted philosophy becomes a lifestyle.[6]

This progression means that thoughts can be extremely powerful and lead to the development of entire cultures—or, at times, the changing of an existing culture. All of creation began as a thought or idea in God's mind, as did the development of every human culture, civilization, invention, and work of art. Think about the influence and impact of ideas:

1. The most powerful force on Earth is an idea.
2. Everything on Earth is the result of an idea.

3. Everything began and begins as an idea.
4. Ideas produce everything.
5. Ideas are more powerful than death.
6. Death cannot kill an idea.
7. Ideas cannot be destroyed.
8. Ideas multiply when attacked.
9. Ideas submerge and reemerge.
10. Ideas are the source of belief.
11. The world is ruled by dead men's ideas.

The kingdom of God was God's big idea from the beginning. It is His powerful thought and provision, and it will change our world into the kingdom of our God. That is why we share the good news. It is as powerful as an idea—and especially so as God's idea.

We must plant the seeds of the idea of the kingdom of God, its government, its community, and its culture. This is the idea and reality that will lead to the belief that will change Earth into the habitation of our King and destroy the works of the enemy. Author H.G. Wells, a noted atheist, historian and author even said, "This is the most revolutionary idea I have ever heard. God replacing the systems of the world with His kingdom." This is exactly His plan. (Hebrews 12; 26-28 TPT)

I once heard pastor and author Jerry Horner use a great illustration of how we relate to the world around us. He said,

> If you place a boat in the water, it will float; but if you put too much water in the boat, it sinks. In the same way, if you put citizens of God's kingdom in the world, they will rise above it; but if you put too much of the world into the citizens of God, they will sink.

As citizens of the kingdom who live under the government of God while also on a mission to bring His heavenly government to bear on Earth, we need to be aware of where we get our beliefs. We must thoroughly ground ourselves in His truth and not be compromised by the values and perspectives of the world around us. We need God's pure, filtered water of life—not the world's tainted waters that lead to destruction.

The Truth about You and God

In the last chapter, we looked at knowing our position in Christ and what He says about us. We also delved into the process of operating from that identity, which includes living in the reality of the law of the spirit of life in Christ instead of the law of sin and death. It is vital to see ourselves as overcomers, as royal priests in the kingdom of God, as strong and victorious, and much more. Who we are will never hold us back, but who we think we are might. If we do not change our mind about our identity and the position, gifts, and blessings God has given us, we will not be able to impact the outcomes in our lives.

We have also looked at who God is and what He wants for us. He is on our side, and He has given us everything we need to live victoriously in the system of His kingdom to have dominion on Earth. We can believe that He is good, that He is a rewarder of those who seek Him, and that He cares enough to provide the wisdom and understanding we need to do what He has called us to do. He will never hold us back, but our false perceptions of Him might. We must trust His Word. In his classic book, *The Knowledge of the Holy*, revered pastor and author A.W. Tozer wrote, "What comes to our minds when we talk about God is the most important thing to us. ... Worship is pure or base as the worshiper entertains high or low thoughts of God."[7]

Many of us are afraid to stand on God's promises because we are afraid those promises will not work. Millions of believers have let too much of the world into their thinking and, as a result, are afraid to say what the Word says because they have been beaten down by the world and its systems. *If it does not work, the world might laugh,* we may be tempted to think. That is why we must write and cash the check of faith.

Some believers may believe in Christ and be redeemed, but they are not in the restoration process. They drank from God's pure waters, but still sip on the polluted waters of the world. The Laodicean church in Revelation comes to mind. Because they had not changed their mindset—they did not fill their mind with the truth that God had put into their spirit—they were "taking on the water" of the world. As a result, their spiritual boats were swamped (to use Horner's analogy). God's revelation to the Apostle John says,

> *I know all the things you do, that you are neither hot nor cold. I wish that you were one or the other! But since you are like lukewarm water, neither hot nor cold, I will spit you out of my mouth!*
>
> —Revelation 3:15-16

Like the boat-swamped believers in Laodicea, it is impossible to live as a kingdom citizen and pursue God's way of doing things if we do not have faith that His way of doing things will accomplish different outcomes in our lives. We must learn to fully believe His promises and cultivate an intimate relationship by spending time with Him in fellowship.

Miracles and the Rule of Heaven

Before we discuss more specifically how we can live a life of miracles, let's review the good news of the kingdom:

1. When God was on Earth as Jesus Christ, He made it clear that His primary message was to teach and declare the kingdom.
2. He clearly told His followers to pray toward that end.
3. He instructed them to begin prayer by honoring the Father who is in heaven and asking Him for His kingdom, His governance, and His way of doing and being right to be manifested on Earth as it is in heaven. He repeatedly declared that this was the Father's will.
4. The earth was to become like the kingdom of heaven. This means that when we are born again by faith, our spirit becomes new. We, then, are citizens of God's kingdom government.
5. God Himself has provided this government and personally delivered it to Earth for all humanity to engage in a life that mirrors that of the kingdom of heaven.
6. Jesus demonstrated this forcefully while living on Earth. He declared that the citizens of His government would do greater things than He had done while He was on Earth (John 14:12)—that they would demonstrate the presence of His power as an inherent part of His kingdom.

Does your life represent the experiences of heaven? Is it really supposed to? Can citizens of the kingdom of God really experience heaven's realities while living on Earth?

Yes, Jesus promised us a life of miracles. A miracle is an unexpected event attributed to divine intervention. I rarely use the word "supernatural"—it is not found in the Scriptures and makes "natural" the standard. The miraculous is not tied to the natural at all.

When we learn to live in the miraculous and accept it as the norm, then we will experience what much of the church and the world calls supernatural. Story after story in Scripture demonstrates God's intervention to enable His people to carry out His plans and fulfill His purposes—which are for us to subdue the earth and reign in dominion over it, much like a colony of heaven.

If what we call "supernatural" is a departure from the natural way things on Earth operate, then we must assume that the way the earth currently operates is natural. It is—for unregenerate human beings who have not encountered God or learned to live in His government system. Jesus and His disciples seemed to disturb the natural ways of the earth, and their disruptions were, now, to be the new natural or "normal" way of life for believers in Jesus, the citizens of His government. Examples of such "holy disturbances" include:

- Jesus healing a blind man by spitting in the dirt and placing the mud in his eyes.
- The power leaving Jesus' body when the woman with the issue of blood touched His garment.
- Jesus calming the storm on the Sea of Galilee.
- Peter walking on the water.
- Five loaves and two fishes multiplying to feed thousands.

- Jesus' first miracle of turning water into fine wine.

Let's look at where this belief about what is natural and what is supernatural comes from. The word "supernatural" tends to conjure thoughts of something very difficult and generally impossible. Only a special, highly trained few can do supernatural things, according to most people's way of thinking. And only rarely can those special few do them.

This viewpoint, however, is untrue and from the kingdom of darkness.

From God's perspective—His way of doing and being right—the supernatural is very natural. Just like it is in heaven. Miracles, which are really departures from the way the kingdom of darkness operates on Earth, are to be commonplace among citizens of the kingdom of God. They are the natural way of the kingdom.

Miracles are the blessings of the will of God delivered by citizen representatives of His government through the Holy Spirit God. They are the demonstration of God's goodness that show lost humanity His plan and His system, which is what lost humanity has been longing for. Remember what Romans 8:19-22 says: all creation desperately longs for the revelation of the sons of God and the day of deliverance. Miracles draw people to salvation and into a relationship with the King. Jesus modeled this time and again during his three-year ministry on Earth.

In the kingdom that God Himself has placed in our spirit, miracles are commonplace, though we often do not recognize them as miracles. Because of the term "supernatural," day-to-day, average, run-of-the-mill miracles are overlooked because they are not dramatic enough. When forced to accept the many miracles that dominate our lives, we often classify them according to an arbitrary sense of sensationalism, much like we rank our shortcomings and sins. In reality, as citizens of the kingdom government of God, our lives are infused with a continual occurrence of miracles.

A friend of mine shared that when he and his wife were young and broke, they were short $514 on their rent one month. They were not sure what to do, so they prayed and asked God for provision. The morning after praying their prayer, a check arrived from their auto insurance company for a refund due to an overcharge error. The amount of the refund? $514.

Of course, if we pay attention, we can see "dramatic" miracles as well. There is a joke that goes like this: "American Christians will pray for healing for a sick friend; they are just surprised if the friend is actually healed." There is truth to that. Our western culture does not give room for the miraculous. We believe such visible demonstrations of God's power are reserved for the mission field. Friends, I have spent a good deal of time in Mexico as a volunteer missions pilot. I can tell you that in places like Latin America, the veil between the kingdom of light and the kingdom of darkness is much thinner, and more believers expect miracles and see them occur.

This is not esoteric magic we are talking about it—some strange, conjured outcome that seeps out of the ether. This power of healing comes from our gracious, caring God who loves us so much that He still moves in miracles. He is *Jehovah-Rapha*, "the God who heals" in Hebrew.

To activate miracles, we need to align our faith and belief with their kingdom reality. When we do, we open ourselves to a greater capacity to see "supernatural" miracles become natural occurrences.

Indeed, when we recognize miracles and thank God for their presence and intervention in our lives, they have the propensity to increase. In the spiritual realm of His kingdom, I believe this is as much a natural law as the law of gravity is in the earthly realm. Think of it this way: if we did not believe in gravity and never tested its existence (e.g., by jumping off a chair or throwing an apple in the air), its reality would remain a theory, right? Sure, every now and then we might accidentally drop our keys and be reminded of gravity, but we would not walk in its daily reality.

The same is true of the miraculous: we must press into what God says and does in His Word; we must believe Jesus—the miracle worker—who said that we would do greater works than Him. When we do, God answers. The more we move from theorizing about miracles to believing in miracles, the greater likelihood and opportunity for us to see them manifest in our lives.

By faithfully acknowledging and honoring God for all the small miracles that happen for us every day, perhaps we would also realize His pledge: if we are faithful in small things, we will be given authority to walk in greater things. We will see greater miracles happen.

Cultivating Miracles

How do we actively cultivate miracles in our lives and experience them each day? Jesus established what the kingdom life offers regarding miracles, both by conduct and by expectation. I do not recall a single record of Jesus having to work up His karma or earn enough holiness to flow naturally in the manifestation of miracles. When people met the condition of faith, His miracles always seemed to come as naturally as sharing a drink of water.

Whatever need was presented, Jesus knew the Father's will and freely delivered the Father's response to the request. He disrupted the natural growth of a tree with no fruit; He violated the dynamics of nature by walking on water; He healed a young girl He had not seen simply because her father had faith. He opened blind eyes, straightened twisted and deformed hands, brought dead people back to life, delivered many who were tormented by evil spirits, and intervened in many other ways. He told His followers they would do the same, and more. There is a pattern and example here that we can follow.

Jesus told His disciples that they were to freely give what they had freely received. He came to destroy the works of the defeated Satan, give His people dominion, and bestow the authority to tread on all the power of the enemy. He sent them out in pairs to deliver the same miracles He had done to those in need and to announce that the kingdom of God had arrived.

We can no longer allow the lies and deceptions of the defeated Satan to shape our understanding or our confession. We must recognize his deceptions and distortions for what they are and from where they come. We must put a stop to them by speaking God's Word in faith and declaring what He has shown to be true.

Miracles, then, are not "supernatural." They are "kingdom natural" and, in fact, show evidence of heaven coming to Earth. They should not be a surprise.

My father had a good friend and mentor in the faith that used to create his own scripture-like sayings or truisms. I have always remembered one of them: "Blessed is the man who expects nothing, for he shall not be disappointed." In many of the miracles we see, if not most of them, there is a real expectancy of the desired results.

In the New Testament, a needy person's ability to get to Jesus to answer their need was usually motivated by the person's recognition of who Jesus was and is. If you look at His miracles throughout the gospels, you will find a good bit of variety between them, but you will also find some consistent themes and principles.

One of those common characteristics was that Jesus viewed miracles as the natural acts of a person in relationship with God the Father through the kingdom. There was no hype, no conjuring up an emotion with music, no rolling on the floor, no shouting as if those around could not hear—just the simple, straightforward verbal declaration of the will of the Father.

Why do many people today believe that something dramatic—or even ridiculous—must occur before the miraculous can intervene? I cannot find any scriptural basis for this approach. The only time we see Jesus raising His voice is in response to spiritual hypocrites or those who turned His Father's temple into a marketplace.

Why do we think miracles are not a normal part of a believer's life? When did we stop believing that the function of citizens of the kingdom is to deliver heaven to Earth? This is one of those areas where we need to examine the source of our beliefs. Earth is where we are meant to rule and reign. We need to find out what Jesus taught and did and make that our belief.

How to Walk in Miracles

Jesus told us how to walk daily in miracles. From His teachings on the matter and His demonstrations of the miraculous, these basic truths emerge:

1. Have faith in God. This is easy to do if you know Him, not if you only know *about* Him. In other words, our faith comes out of our relationship with Him. Relationship comes from fellowship; fellowship comes from time spent together, and time spent together comes from a commitment to give the time. I shared the following illustration earlier, but it is worth re-emphasizing: my wife and I have been married for more than fifty years. Consider what would have happened if, on our wedding day, I had delivered Fran to a place I had prepared especially for her and said, "Honey, I will visit you for a couple hours on Sundays. I will not fellowship with you, but I will listen to what other people say about you. Some weeks I will also do that on Wednesdays. When I need you to perform for me, I want you to be ready to respond instantly, whatever the need is." I am confident this arrangement would not have worked with Fran, and I am even more positive it does not work with God. He is a God of relationship, not shortcuts.

2. Know and speak the will of God for each need. In every situation, circumstance, and relationship, we can gain the knowledge and understanding of His will and establish it in our mind through our fellowship with the Father and the prompting of the Spirit. We allow the Word of God to change the way we think. We no longer think as the world thinks. God responds not to need but to seed. We need to discern His word for the situation and speak it in faith. His Word is the seed we plant.

3. Attack doubt. We cannot allow doubt to enter our knowledge of the will of God. Doubt is negative faith—faith in an alternate outcome that is not God's will. It is scary to listen to many citizens of the kingdom and hear where their faith is placed. "I cannot deliver miracles. That is for people especially chosen by God—people with a special gift, not ordinary people like me. I cannot pray in faith for your healing because I am not sure it is God's will for you to be healed. Sickness might be God's will for now." And on and on. We must know and understand the plan and will of God and believe it without doubting. We do not "perform" miracles; we are citizens of the kingdom who deliver them through our knowledge and understanding of the system Jesus placed on Earth for us to operate in right now. We position ourselves and the Holy Spirit works through us. Does this mean we will never experience doubt or fear? Of course not. But when those emotions drive us away from God's purposes, we take them captive and surrender them to the Lord.

4. Pray and believe we have already received God's answer. The three faithful Hebrews—Shadrach, Meshach, and Abednego—all survived Nebuchadnezzar's furnace because they knew the miracle-working God (Daniel 3). They understood His power and provision. They saw the outcome and defeated any existing doubts or fears. We must know that God produces the desires of our spirit and mind by our fellowship with Him. As we have deep fellowship with Him, our thoughts become agreeable with His thoughts, and our will becomes agreeable with His will. Our plans are established, and they succeed.

5. Forgive. There can be no unforgiveness in our spirit or mind. In all the years of ministry that Fran and I have been privileged to take part in, one common factor among people who struggle to find healing and restoration is the inability to forgive. Unforgiveness stops the flow of miracles. As you seek to forgive others, do not belabor the past and drag up every memory of every offense. Only address what the Holy Spirit brings to your memory and your thoughts. Make a conscious decision to forgive and take all your unforgiveness to God in prayer. At times, He will guide you to either go in person or, if that is not possible, reach out directly to ask forgiveness of someone you may have wronged or hurt in the past or someone who has hurt you. Follow His Word and the direction of the Spirit—they will agree and never steer you incorrectly.

6. Expect miracles continuously. Look and listen for situations where you can be used to birth the kingdom into the lives of others by delivering the kingdom-natural will of the Father into their need. I love the analogy of the Israelites standing on the walls, watching and expectant (see Isaiah 62:6-7.) We must do the same—seeking God's kingdom for those who need His healing and restoration. Do not make the process spooky or super spiritual or turn it into a religious act. Do not buy into the "other guy syndrome" and expect that assignment from God to be for someone else. Chances are, if God puts someone on your heart, He wants to use you as His vessel for healing.

Know that you are ready, willing, and able to walk in this reality with your God. He is the true and living God. He is the only wise God. His plans and provisions for us are not lacking. We have not been shorted. We have the relationship of power all humanity is searching for. Our relationship with Him is the "if" or the discipline part of the conditional statement, and the results are the "then." If we are living in a right relationship with Him, then we can experience the outcomes we are meant to experience. We must show God's praises by our acts and works until Jesus returns. Through His goodness, expressed through us, He draws people to salvation and into a relationship with Him.

Do Not Turn Back

Where are you right now? What challenges are you facing? Is everything in your life great—no clouds in the sky? Or are you in the heat of an intense battle?

Your efforts to walk in miracles will not be unopposed. The modus operandi of the defeated Satan has not changed. Be encouraged. The more the heat increases, the more proof he is giving you that you are very close to victory. Our victory is the place where our God shows up, makes His presence known, and confirms His Word and our faith through a miraculous manifestation.

There is never a time for surrender. We must stand fast and dispatch the Angel Armies of God to create the right circumstances, situations, and relationships that allow the Word of God to be manifested in our lives, just as He has declared.

One of the greatest challenges of my life has been when I have tried to explain why my experience was not lining up with God's description of what it is supposed to be. Remember that our God does not lie. He says what He means and means what He says. He has done and will continue to do exactly what He has said.

Wherever you are on your journey as a kingdom citizen, you are more than a conqueror through Christ (Romans 8:37); you are made to triumph in every situation in Him (2 Corinthians 2:14), and the One living in you and working through you is greater than he who is working in the world (1 John 4:4). No weapon formed against you will prosper (Isaiah 54:17). When your enemies come at you from one direction, God will send them scattering in seven (Deuteronomy 28:7). Whenever you call upon the name of the Lord, you will be saved (Romans 10:13).

Why do all of us seemingly experience defeat and frustration at times? The defeated Satan creates a diversion, and we get so busy putting out fires that we neglect to do battle in the spirit world. The physical world is much more visible, and our eyes are drawn to the manifestation of some form of deception. Whether that deception appears as a situation, a circumstance, or a relationship, it seems overwhelming. It may look like an out-of-control fire, a massive tsunami, or just a little lie that someone started. The manifestation may be real, but its power is not.

No power is greater than God's or the innate power of His kingdom that He has placed within us. We have access to all the power of heaven. We are instructed to call heaven to Earth to intervene in all our situations, circumstances, and relationships that are in conflict with what God has said.

My family and I have been through very intense battles over the years. Around the time I first wrote this book (2012), things were particularly intense. Some of our advisors encouraged us to give up and admit that the challenges and adversaries were bigger than us—that they could outlast and outspend us. Those giants were visibly stronger than we were, but in the end, we prevailed. Not in the way, perhaps, that I had envisioned but in the way God ordained it to be. We held to our positions as kingdom citizens, and God was glorified. That is the way this works.

Does that sound familiar? It is the same situation the Israelites faced before they entered the Promised Land. Moses had to remind the people that even though the giants were big, God would cross the Jordan River ahead of them like a devouring fire to destroy the enemy. He would drive them out, just as He promised. (See Deuteronomy 9.)

Just like Israel, our participation in the battle will be required. We will have to engage the enemy, but we can also be confident that our victory is in the presence of God. He is with us. He has said He will never leave us or forsake us. He will go with us to the ends of the earth. As we declare His Word to be true, sure, steadfast, and eternal, we will see it manifesting in our lives and the world around us.

There is a canvas in our minds where we paint the picture of our faith for our Creator God to fulfill. When Jesus was on the earth as Emmanuel, God with us, He perfectly modeled and presented the actions and results of our engaging the redemptive Kingdom of our God for our governance. His example displays how we are to address all of our situations, our circumstances, and our relationships. We through the currency of our faith paint the picture on our canvas that mirrors His actions.

1. How did He address sickness? He healed them all.
2. How did He address shortage? He multiplied what was there, and there was more left over after meeting the need than when they began. Widow's oil, loaves and fish, wine.
3. How did He address lack? He engaged Heaven's realm and called into the Earth realm what was needed. Gold in fish mouth, ram for Abraham and Isaac, fish for disciples.
4. How did He address unclean spirits? He recognized them and directed them to leave those they were tormenting.
5. How did He address things that were threatening people in the earth? He calmed the storm by engaging the more powerful realm of Heaven.

Whatever situation, circumstance, or relationship we encounter in the earth, we have been charged to engage Heaven and to call Heaven to the earth. Without fear and without doubt we can and must act upon everything as Jesus did. He has provided the established precedents and they are in our Constitution. We must paint that picture on the canvas in our minds for the Holy Spirit God to fulfill. He is the author and the finisher of our faith. He completes what we believe and present for Him.

We must declare our faith vision out loud verbally. This activates all of the forces of Heaven's realm to accomplish the vision we have received from our God. What an amazing honor we have to deliver and to declare His will to the earth to honor Him and to bless humanity. This is our mission and our charge.

YOUR DECLARATIONS

KNOW WHAT YOU BELIEVE

Praying through a passage of Scripture is a powerful experience. We can be confident that it is consistent with God's will because it is His Word to us. My family often prays Isaiah 58 over our lives:

Father God, (list your name and your family members' names here), all of our heirs and all of our descendants forever: We forever declare our allegiance and our passion for Your Word. We will shout with a loud voice, proclaiming loudly Your goodness, and tell everyone of Your worthiness to be praised continually.

We commit our lives to obey Your Word and to follow Your instructions. We work to free those who are wrongly imprisoned. We lighten the burdens of those who work with us in the fields of labor that You have given to us. We secure freedom for those who are oppressed by the kingdom of darkness. We remove the chains that bind humanity. We share the food from our table with those who are hungry. We provide shelter to those who are without homes. We give clothing to those in need. We do not hide from our relatives who are in need.

Because we obey Your commands and because we walk in Your ways, our salvation is as dependable as the dawn. Our salvation is sure, and our salvation is trustworthy. Our wounds heal quickly, Lord. You, Father God, have given us Your godliness to lead us forward, and Your glory protects us from behind.

When we call out to You, Lord, You answer quickly and declare that You are always present to hear and to answer our petitions and requests. You do so Lord, quickly and lavishly.

Your light, Holy Spirit God, shines brightly out of our spirit into the darkness that is around us, and that darkness becomes as bright as the noon sun. You, Holy Spirit, guide us continually; You saturate us with water when we are dry. You abundantly restore our strength. We are like well-watered gardens and ever-flowing springs.

We rebuild the walls of our cities for protection. We restore the deserted ruins of our cities and the homes that have been battered and torn by the deceits of the defeated Satan.

We maintain our relationship with You, Father, through continual fellowship. We spend time with You, Father; You are our delight and our heart's desire. Nothing that we desire compares to our passion for You. We live, we walk, and we have our being in the wonderful inheritance you have graciously provided to us through relationship. You bring great honor to us, Lord God.

We declare with a loud voice Your goodness. We shout loudly about Your Faithfulness, and we loudly proclaim Your unfailing mercy. We shout praises to Your name continually, forever.

You are the true and living God, the only wise God, our Father. There is no other God. Glory, honor, power, praises, and dominion continually be to You, now and forevermore. Amen.

All of the declarations found here, and many more, are available in the book Kingdom Activating Declarations by Charlie Lewis.

Visit www.ksam.net for this and other great resources.

CHAPTER 8

THE VOICE OF A KINGDOM CITIZEN

The tongue can bring death or life;
those who love to talk will reap the consequences.

—Proverbs 18:21

After Fran and I held the "Going Out of Business" sale for the furniture business, we took some time off. We left our two sons with her parents in Florida and took an amazing trip to Israel. Then, we came back to the States, through New York, where we met up with our sons and Fran's parents. There, in New York, we decided to drive back to Georgia, the highlight being the Blue Ridge Parkway. It is a scenic road that winds along the spine of the Blue Ridge Mountains through the states of Virginia and North Carolina.

When we reached Tennessee, we were reminded of an earlier visit to the same area and an amazing demonstration of God's kingdom at work. During that previous trip, we had stopped for a bite to eat. While

I was backing out, I dinged the car next to us, leaving a small dent. I went back into the restaurant and asked whose car it was, but no one seemed to know. I decided to write a note on the back of one of my business cards, placed it under the wiper blade, and got back on the road.

At this time, Fran and I were continuing to seek God's direction for the next season of our lives. I had forgotten about the car incident in Tennessee when a couple of weeks later I received a phone call. Here is the amazing part of this story: as it turned out, the owner of the vehicle was a local doctor, and he and his family lived in Thomasville. We were from the same town of 20,000 in southwestern Georgia, and his was the car I happened to ding in a restaurant parking lot some 500 miles away in Tennessee.

"What are the odds?" you might ask. But in God's kingdom, odds and luck are not part the equation, as you will see. There is no word for coincidence in the Hebrew language. The physician and his wife turned out to be lovely people who we became friends with over time. One day, he called me and asked if Fran and I would join them for dinner.

Once we were all settled at our table, the gentleman turned to me and said, "Charlie, I want my wife to join me in my business, and we want you and Fran to buy our jewelry store." Fran and I could have fallen out of our chairs; we did not know anything about the jewelry business.

After exchanging a confirming look from Fran, I said, "That is thoughtful of you, but we are going to decline. We do not have the money to buy a jewelry store right now, and we do not have any experience with that." I thought that was the end of it, but God had other plans.

Like the persistent widow who keeps returning to make her pleas to the king, he would not give up. And as Fran and I prayed about it, we finally came around to the idea of purchasing their store—even though we knew only the furniture business, which is very different from selling jewelry.

From there, the divine doors flew open. To begin with, the agreement was completely verbal—which is an example of how important words are in God's kingdom. Before I knew it, we had secured a loan, bought the business, and the gentleman graciously financed the down payment. Fran embarked on a steep curve to learn the jewelry business and eventually became a graduate gemologist, an international certified diamond appraiser, and a leader in her industry. From that one store, the businesses grew. Fast forward some forty-plus years, and we owned fifteen stores from Texas to Colorado to Alabama to Georgia and Florida.

It all started with a verbal agreement and a handshake with a doctor that we would never have met if I had not been distracted while backing out of a restaurant parking spot in the middle of Tennessee. Coincidence? No way. Though we did not yet fully understand the full picture of God's kingdom at that time, we did realize that this was a divine appointment. God knew ahead of time what He had planned for us. Fran calls this type of experience the "opportunity of integrity."

Words are powerful. And when we speak the word in love and truth and are fully walking in His kingdom, words can become the devices that allow us to leverage things that we otherwise could not possibly achieve—to do things that we otherwise would never be able to do. If someone would have told Fran and me that someday we would own more than a dozen jewelry stores, we both would have laughed.

But for God, all things are possible.

The Power of a Kingdom Citizen's Words

The words of a kingdom believer hold power. They can be so powerful that silence is often the wiser option. Not many people realize that, as evidenced by how casually people speak careless sayings, clichés, pointed comments, and clever but harmful quips. The world is full of such sayings, and most people seem to be convinced that they have no real effect. We laugh at them and continue with our lives.

Where do these words come from? Words are simply ideas or thoughts that are expressed through language in songs, books, movies, television, church, conversations with friends and family, among many other sources. If you have ever caught yourself singing a song and suddenly understood the idea that the words are really communicating and then gasping at what is coming out of your mouth—you know how easy it is to repeat things without thinking about them.

Look at just a few of the things Scripture says about the power of our words:

> *The tongue is a small thing that makes grand speeches. But a tiny spark can set a great forest on fire. The tongue is a flame of fire. It is a whole world of wickedness, corrupting your entire body. It can set your whole life on fire, for it is set on fire by hell itself.*
>
> —James 3:5, 6

> *You brood of snakes. How could evil men like you speak what is good and right? For whatever is in your heart determines what you say. A good person produces good things from the treasury of a good heart; an evil person produces evil things from the treasury of an evil heart. And I tell you*

> *this; you must give an account on judgment day for every idle word you speak. The words you say will either acquit you or condemn you.*
>
> —Matthew 12:34-37

> *May the words of my mouth and the meditation of my heart be pleasing to you.*
>
> —Psalms 19:14

> *The tongue can bring death or life; those who love to talk will reap the consequences.*
>
> —Proverbs 18:21

> *I tell you the truth, you can say to this mountain, "May you be lifted up and thrown into the sea," and it will happen. But you must really believe it will happen and have no doubt in your heart.*
>
> —Mark 11:23

So, are words just words? Does what comes out of our mouths really matter? Are words just harmless, meaningless sounds that have no effect on our surroundings? Look at what famed pastor and author Jack Hayford said:

> It is a phenomenal truth. Everything that exists came about by words. In the most deterministic chapter in the Bible pertaining to our world—Chapter One of the book of Genesis—we read that God spoke, and all things came into being: "God said . . . and it was so.

> God called . . . and it was good. Then God blessed . . ." (verses 3, 7, 10, 28). It is the verbal activity of Almighty God that literally decrees our world's existence.[8]

How does this relate to those who are created in God's image and likeness? Consider this:

1. We are made from the same substance as our Creator.
2. We are told that whatever we allow, lock, or bind on Earth will be allowed, locked, or bound in heaven (Matthew 16:19).
3. If God's words are powerful and effective, and we are made in His likeness, that means our words are meant to be powerful and effective, too.

Dr. Pepe Ramnath, a scientist, pastor, teacher, and expositor of God's Word, examined Jesus' statement that whatever we bind or loose on Earth will be bound or loosed in heaven. The earth refers to our environment, and the heavens refer to the atmosphere that surrounds Earth. This may be a little different than many of us have heard before, but consider Dr. Ramnath's findings:

1. The environment of Earth affects and controls the atmosphere of the heavenlies.
2. The atmosphere is where all the influence of our environment is determined and constructed. An atmosphere is controlled by what goes into it.
3. According to the dynamics and principles of the

> environment, nothing happens in the atmosphere until the environment gives it the right gases and energy.

Based on these scientific principles, we understand that what we say can and does impact our atmosphere (i.e., the invisible realm surrounding us), and what we place in our atmosphere controls what happens in our environment. It is a cyclical dynamic whereby we influence the heavenly places, which in turn influence the environment around us.

In Scripture, we see that the atmosphere around Earth has significant impact on Earth. Jesus was saying that as His followers, we in the kingdom government, kingdom culture, and kingdom community have authority over our atmosphere. We determine the atmospheric effect of our environment. Whatever we allow and declare on Earth *creates* our atmosphere. Our atmosphere creates our environment according to what we have allowed and declared.

What We Empower

Because of this ability to impact our atmosphere and therefore our environment, we need to be very mindful of our words. Whose thoughts or ideas are they confirming? To whom are we giving the authority to develop the atmosphere that creates our environment? Religion concentrates on getting everyone to heaven, but Jesus taught us that we are to bring heaven to Earth. Jesus taught that the proper position for a believer is to be in relationship with Him so we can experience the benefits of His kingdom on the earth as citizens of that kingdom.

We are people in conflict. The theology of the church is generally in conflict with the theology of the Scriptures. That is not true for all churches at all times, but for most of Christian history, and for most churches today, it is true. The kingdom is not highlighted in most of our creeds, even though it is the foundation for all scriptural revelation. If we do not understand the kingdom, we cannot correctly interpret and apply God's Word. This is the main subject throughout the Scriptures.

We must capture every thought and imagination that is contrary to the kingdom teachings of Jesus and bring them all into submission to and alignment with His Word. As we have seen in this book so far, we will know His ideas through relationship with Him. We cultivate relationship with Him through fellowship with Him, and we have fellowship with Him by spending time with Him. We will then know His voice and understand His will and His Word.

This is exactly what happened to Fran and me regarding our divine appointment with the local doctor and his wife and how we entered the jewelry industry. We were passionately pursuing His place and purpose for us and walking in agreement with His kingdom principles. We are flawed human beings, for sure, but we had the faith to believe for His answer. Put differently, we were asking the questions in faith, and He provided the answers—clearly and powerfully. This, again, is Fran's opportunity of integrity—when we walk in faith and listen to His instructions, our integrity in doing so opens doors of opportunity.

As we recognize the Father's voice, we understand His motivations, purposes, plans, principles, and actions. When we do this—align with His truth and know what He is doing and saying—we must then line up our words with His words and become creators of our environment, just as He spoke into the darkness and created the universe. This is our role as those created in His image.

Our words create the environment in which we live and function every day. The words we speak change the atmosphere and cause it to create a kingdom culture and a kingdom governance experience. We are neither helpless nor hopeless. We are in charge of our environment. Our confession must agree and align with the words of our King.

Jesus modeled this for us when He spoke to a fruitless fig tree and ordered that no one would ever eat of its fruit again. The next morning, the disciples noticed that the tree had withered and died. They remembered Jesus's words from the day before, and He told them that they could speak to mountains and command them to move—if they believed with all their heart the words they were speaking (Mark 11:12-14, 20-25). The picture was painted on the canvas in their minds. Clearly, Jesus was not demonstrating a privilege that was exclusive to Him as God's Son. He taught His followers that they could do the same thing with the words they speak. Faith is the currency of His kingdom.

We can be free from frustration. We can recognize the strategies and deceits of the defeated enemy and put a stop to them by speaking the words of our God in faith. We are not passive victims of our circumstances, situations, and relationships. We will encounter adversity, but we have the authority to shape how it impacts us so we can overcome it. We are to become shapers of our environment through the authority we have been given in our words.

When you know God's motivations, purposes, plans, principles, and actions, you can speak His will into the circumstances, situations, and relationships of your life—not to be a selfish manipulator, but to be the selfless kingdom citizen you were created to be and to bring heaven to Earth.

Faith That Overcomes

You can begin speaking many truths into your environment today. You may have to seek and discover God's thoughts on some matters before you know what to declare, but you can already confidently declare those truths that are clearly laid out in His Word. Many believe they know the Word of God, but their life experiences show that they know only words. Here are a few clear truths you could start with, and more extensive confessions are included at the end of this chapter. Say these out loud, along with any other truths you find in His Word:

- Greater are You who is living in and working through me than he that is in the world (1 John 4:4).
- We take our shield of faith, and we quench the adversary's every fiery dart (Ephesians 6:16).
- Our God keeps us in perfect peace because our mind stays on Him, and because we trust Him (Isaiah26:3).
- We can and we do all things through Christ who strengthens us (Philippians 4:13).
- We are crucified with Christ; it is no longer we who live but Christ who lives in us (Galatians 2:20).
- Whatever we bind on earth will be bound in heaven, and whatever we loose on earth will be loosed in heaven (Matthew 16:19).
- God forgives all of our sin. He heals all of our diseases. He redeems our lives from the pit. He crowns us with faithful love and compassion. He satisfies us with goodness. He renews our youth like the eagle (Psalm 103:1-5).
- Whatever we ask for in prayer, we believe we have received it. It is ours (Mark 11:24).

Go back through each of those truths and think specifically about how your life and your environment would be changed if each one was fully manifested in your life, then paint that picture on your canvas. Use a separate piece of paper or journal to capture your thoughts. Why are they not experiential realities for most people? Even when we believe these truths in our heart, our words do not always reflect what we say we believe. We speak forth ideas and expectations that contradict what Scripture tells us is true. Often, we reap the harvest of the seeds we have sown with our words, and we experience realities we do not want to experience.

Begin to change that today. Determine whose words you will confess and declare in your conversations, in the songs you sing, and in the praises you lift up. Whatever situation you find yourself in, declare the truth over that situation and refuse to be moved. Pray, declare, claim promises from the Word, let that be the picture on your canvas, and stand on what you know to be true.

Invite the Holy Spirit into the situation, and give Him full access. Do not deny the adversity and challenges you are facing, but do deny their ability to control and impact the situation you are in. Rejecting them is different from denying them. Do not utter any words of doubt or falsehood, but only words full of faith, truth, hope, and love. If you are new to this process of speaking declarations, read the Scriptures out loud. Let your speech overflow with expectation of God's goodness. Then, watch your environment conform to His will.

YOUR DECLARATIONS

CHANGE YOUR ENVIRONMENT

Father God, (list your name and your family members' names here), all of our heirs and all of our descendants forever, we declare that You, as the Lord Jesus Christ, are Lord over our spirit, our mind, and our body. (Philippians 2:9-11)

Jesus, You are made unto us to be wisdom, righteousness, sanctification, redemption, and the full restoration of the Kingdom System of our God in our lives, both in relationship and in practical benefit. We can and we do all things through You, Lord Jesus. You are our strength. (1 Corinthians 1:30; Philippians 4:13)

Lord, You are our Shepherd, we do not want. You, Father God, supply all our need according to Your riches in glory in Christ Jesus. Your glory is all around us, and we reach out into Your Kingdom (Heaven's realm) and pull into ourselves all that we need in every area of our lives. (Psalm 23; Philippians 4:19)

We do not fret or have anxiety about anything. We do not have a care. (Philippians 4:6, 1 Peter 5:6, 7)

We are the Body of Christ. We are redeemed from the curse because you, Lord Jesus, bore our sickness, and You carried our disease in Your own body. By your stripes we are healed. We forbid any sickness or any virus to operate in our body.

Every organ, every tissue, every fiber, and every cell of our being functions in the perfection in which You, Father God, created it to function. We honor You, God, and bring glory to You in our bodies. (Galatians 3:13; Matthew 8:17; 1 Peter 2:24)

We have the mind of Christ Jesus, and we hold the thoughts, the feelings, and the purposes of Your Spirit and Your mind. (1 Corinthians 2:16)

We are believers, not doubters. We hold fast to our confession of faith. We decide to walk by faith and to practice faith. Our faith comes from hearing Your Word, Lord Jesus. Jesus, You are the author and developer of our faith, the One who finishes and completes our faith. (Hebrews 4:14; 11:6; Romans 10:17)

Your love, Father God, has been poured out in our spirit and into our mind by the Holy Spirit God, and Your love dwells in us continually and richly. We keep ourselves in the kingdom of light, in Your love, and in the Word, and the wicked one touches us not. (Romans 5:5; 1 John 4:6)

We tread upon serpents and scorpions and over all power of the enemy. We take our shield of faith, and we quench every fiery dart of the defeated Satan. Greater are You, Lord God, who lives in and works through us than he who is in the world. (Psalm 91:13; Ephesians 6:16; 1 John 4:4; 5:18)

We are delivered from this present evil world. We are seated with you, Christ Jesus, in heavenly places. We reside in the kingdom of God's dear Son. The law of the spirit of life in Christ Jesus has made us free from the law of sin and death. (Galatians 1:4; Ephesians 2:6; Colossians 1:13; Romans 8:2)

We do not fear because you, Father God, have given us the spirit of power, and your love, and we operate from a sound mind. God, You are on our side. (2 Timothy 1:7; Romans 8:31)

We hear and we recognize the voice of the Good Shepherd. We hear and we know our Father's voice, and the voice of a stranger we will not follow. We roll our works upon You, Lord Jesus. We commit, and we trust them completely to You. You cause our thoughts to become agreeable with Your will so are our plans established and our plans succeed. (John 10:27; Proverbs 16:3)

We are world overcomers, Father God, because we are born of You. We represent the Father and Jesus's will. We are useful members of the body of Christ. We are Your workmanship, Father God, recreated in Christ Jesus. You, Father God, are continually and effectively at work in us to lead us to want to do, and then to do, Your good pleasure. (1 John 5:4–5; Ephesians 2:10; Philippians 2:13)

We let your Word dwell in us richly. You have begun a good work in us, and You will continue it until the day of Your reappearing.

Praise be to Your name, our Father. You are always faithful and we are always thankful.

All of the declarations found here, and many more, are available in the book Kingdom Activating Declarations by Charlie Lewis.

Visit www.ksam.net for this and other great resources.

CHAPTER 9

LIVING IN KINGDOM POWER

Our doctor friend handed us several sets of keys, then told me that the large property was ours. Fran and I were in shock—the terms of agreement had not yet been finalized; no papers had been signed. This was 1997, and Fran and I were about to embark on an incredible new adventure—owning, renovating, and running a historic plantation near Thomasville.

But, I am getting ahead of myself. Let's go back to where we left off in our story—many years earlier.

The Opportunity of Integrity

Though we held the GOB sale for the furniture business, I still had not heard from the Lord about my next business endeavor. By the way, sometimes an answer from the Lord does not come immediately. We waited and prayed. Approximately one year before, our jewelry opportunity became available. Fran was studying for her diamond appraiser certification by night after putting our two young sons to bed.

At the time, we were part of a wonderful congregation called New Covenant Church in Thomasville, Georgia. Our pastor, Jim Armstrong, was a wonderful spirit-filled man of God who had been dismissed by his former church after he became baptized in the Spirit. Soon after he received the "the left foot of fellowship," he started New Covenant Church. Jim was a tall, lanky guy who had been a B-17 pilot in WWII. During the war, he was shot down over occupied France. He was taken in and hidden by the French Underground with a French family. They were able to get him to the English Channel where he was able to escape back to England.

It was an incredible time at our church, as people were being saved, and many were healed of addictions and diseases. The church's motto is, "Love, Mend, Train, Send." It truly was—and still is—a kingdom-minded church. While it was an incredible season for the church in America, it was also a very difficult time. The nation was hit by a savings and loan crisis that caused interest rates to spike, inflation to rise, as well as unemployment to increase. As interest rates topped twenty percent, it was a crazy time in history.

Though we sold the furniture store nearly a year earlier, we kept the property. Fran began to throw herself into the jewelry business as I sought the Lord for my next business move. I had an office downtown at our building, and a steady flow of people would stop by to visit, talk, and pray. By this time, we had been in Thomasville for several years and had made many friends. We held many incredible prayer meetings in that office, and it became a kind of gathering place.

One day, Pastor Jim dropped by to chat. He got right to the point. "Charlie, I've been praying. This Savings & Loan Crisis has been a disaster for many of our families. Businesses are dropping like flies, and a lot of people in the church are out of work." He paused, then said, "I believe you need to go into the insurance business and put these men in our church to work so they can make a living for their families."

I replied, "Jim, I have never been in the insurance business. I do not know anything about it. I am not interested in that at all, but I will pray about it." Of course, my saying "I will pray about it" was the same as saying, "Sure, Jim."

About a week or so later, Jim dropped by again. "Charlie, I've been praying about it. I really think you need to go into the insurance business so the folks who have lost jobs can make a living for their families." I sat and listened politely. This happened about a year after we closed the furniture store, and I still had not received a clear answer from God about my next move. This time, I *did* take time to pray about what Jim said.

He came back a third time, but this time I felt the conviction of the Holy Spirit. I remember that this was also right before the grand opening of the first jewelry store that we had purchased. As I prayed about Jim's words, the Lord confirmed through a dream that he wanted me to start an insurance business. So I went into the insurance business by the recommendation of my pastor and the prompting of the Holy Spirit. I got my insurance license, started cold-calling potential clients, and hired my first employees.

Fast forward several decades, and God took that persistent prompting from Pastor Jim and turned it into an international insurance company. We are one of the largest family-owned insurance businesses in the senior life and health sector in the nation. We are in all fifty states and have worked with more than 25,000 representatives.

As I say that, I almost have to laugh because I never saw myself as an insurance person. As I re-read the last couple of paragraphs, I know I run the risk of sounding boastful or arrogant. But let me tell you, that is not my intent or position because the success we have had (in the world's terms) is solely because of the Lord taking Fran and me—two broken but willing vessels—and using us to do what He has told us to do.

I mean, look at the pattern of our lives:

- Though I was eligible for draft deferment, I became a pilot and an airfield commander in Southeast Asia.
- We were living an officer's lifestyle, with all the perks and advantages that it offered, but God had us walk away and start from the beginning in the lowest income per capita area of Jacksonville.
- Once we began to thrive there, including the Holy Spirit God growing our youth group to several hundred young people, He had us walk away and go start over in southwest Georgia. A new town, new business, newborn baby, yet we knew no one in Thomasville.
- After we bought our own furniture business and enjoyed amazing growth, the Lord had us not just sell it but made us hold a going out of business sale. (That was quite the humbling experience—and a major leap forward for us in our understanding of how the kingdom operates.)
- Once we returned from our time in Israel, I "happened" to be in a town in Tennessee where I dinged the car of a family that lived in Thomasville, who a number of years later would convince us to buy their jewelry business—an industry we knew nothing about.
- God had to pursue me more than three times and used Pastor Jim to deliver the message I did

> not want to hear: leave the furniture business you have worked in your entire life and start an insurance company.

There is one more huge "kingdom vocation move" that happened to us, which I will get to in a moment. First, as I review that short history of our career moves, what I see is the signature and prints of the Holy Spirit God everywhere. Throughout these pages, I have done the best I can to relay exactly how God moved in each "life change" Fran and I went through. In each one, He always did three things:

1. Continuously took us out of our comfort zone into the unknown.
2. Opened miraculous doors that we could not have opened on our own.
3. Showed us just enough of the "next steps" to keep us dependent upon Him and His voice.

The common denominator in each of these factors is God's kingdom power and direction. The more we came to understand the economy of His kingdom, the more we were able to get out of the way and let Him "rule and reign" in our lives. It is exactly as John the Baptist said about the coming of Jesus:

> *It is necessary for him to increase and for me to decrease. For the one who is from the earth belongs to the earth and speaks from the natural realm. But the One who comes from above is above everything and speaks of the highest realm of all!*
>
> —John 3:30-31 (TPT)

John the Baptist—the cousin of Jesus—got it. He understood his position in the kingdom of God. Even in the womb, upon hearing about his aunt Mary's divine conception of the future Messiah, he leapt in his mother, Elizabeth's, womb. God's kingdom is celebrated and recognized by John, even while still in his mother's womb!

Note that John did not shrink away like a wallflower and say, "I can just chill and stand by the side now that Jesus is here." His prayer for Jesus to increase and him to decrease was about position, not passion. In other words, John remained fully engaged with the kingdom, preaching about the coming Messiah, the Gospel, and the kingdom until his last breath of life.

If I had to summarize the Kingdom System and dynamics into one defining word, it would be this:

Eternality (noun): the quality or state of being eternal

When we live in eternality, we live in a state where our spirit lives and works in the kingdom of God "on earth as it is in heaven." We view business through a lens of eternality; we view family, marriage, friendships, and faith through the lens of eternality. We can operate today in our greatest gifts and strengths because the barriers that keep most people hindered by the kingdom of darkness have been expelled—it is as if we have literally started walking in a heavenly state or realm—now, here on Earth. This clearly is our Creator God's desire and plan for us.

This is not to suggest that we are somehow better than other people. Far from it. It simply means that we understand that the environment here on Earth that we live in, that we work in, and that we worship in are eternal, and we are eternal. It means that through a revelation and a knowledge of His eternality, we "get it"—we get His Kingdom

System, we grasp the eternality of His realm and rule on the earth as it is in heaven.

Living As If Heaven Is Real and Present

In practical terms, living in a mindset of eternality means we have access to the Holy Spirit God's wisdom and power—now. It means we do not have to be burdened down with the world's laws, rules, and compliance tests. So how does one move into a spiritual position of looking at the world through a lens of eternality?

On top of America's seemingly inexorable slide toward secularism, many born-again Christians are struggling in their ability to appropriate the riches and benefits of God's kingdom "on earth as it is in heaven." I believe it is safe to say that most people ask the question, "Is there more than this?" Still, I am not shocked to hear born-again believers asking this same question.

In other words, even after believing in Christ, being redeemed, and living faithfully as a believer in Jesus, they are uncertain about how the here and now relates to the afterlife, their forever hereafter. As a result, I believe many Christians are not experiencing the power and the promises of Scripture as fully as they expected. They realize something is missing.

Maybe you have felt that way. Perhaps you have wondered if there is more to life for a believer and follower of Jesus Christ than you have been experiencing. Maybe you have been searching for that missing piece.

When Paul traveled to Ephesus, he encountered a group of people who believed the message of Jesus and were living in relationship with God through faith (see Acts 19:1-7). Paul considered them to be followers of Jesus; each of their spirits had been made alive by God's Spirit.

They were born again. But Paul did not assume that they were fully experiencing what God had provided. He asked them if they had received the Holy Spirit since they believed.

The timing of his question is interesting. Paul is clearly saying that entrance into God's kingdom does not mean fully experiencing and engaging in all the kingdom benefits. This leads to questions like: "When someone is born again, is it all-encompassing? Is that all there is? Or are there other, subsequent experiences, relationships, or benefits available to followers of Jesus?" The answer to those questions seems clear in Scripture. Just as it is possible to be born of God's Spirit without receiving the indwelling of the Holy Spirit God, it is also possible to enter God's kingdom without living as a kingdom citizen.

At the beginning of my relationship with God the Father through Jesus as my Lord, my response would have been very similar to these followers from Ephesus. I had never heard of a word of knowledge, a word of wisdom, casting out demons, speaking in tongues (the kingdom language); or the kingdom of God with its principles, dynamics, commands, and many experiences. In other words, I was unfamiliar with the realities of eternality.

I first encountered these realities years ago when we were experiencing an outpouring of the Holy Spirit God in meetings we had among our youth group in Jacksonville (before we made the move to Thomasville). For more than a year, we would gather every evening to worship and praise God and listen to the Word being taught. The Holy Spirit would lead the meetings, and we would sing, laugh, cry, pray, shout loudly, and worship softly.

People were healed and set free from the bondages of evil. Addictions were broken; evil spirits left, and many other demonstrations occurred. We did not label these events because we did not know what to call them! Irish playwright George Bernard Shaw once famously quipped, "Youth is the most precious thing in life; it is too bad it has to be wasted on young folks." And while Fran and I were only in our early twenties, and the youth in our group ranged from pre-teen to teen (and even some in their early twenties), I believe God delighted in our exuberance, passion for His Word, and in our hunger to see His power demonstrated through our simple faith. Even though we did not know the proper labels, God's movement was real, and we experienced and enjoyed Him wholeheartedly.

I can also recall times when my religious mindset came creeping back and started getting in the way of what God's Spirit wanted to do. This happened with the Ephesians, too:

> *Some became stubborn, rejecting his message and publicly speaking against the Way. So Paul left the synagogue and took the believers with him. Then he held daily discussions at the lecture hall of Tyrannus.*
>
> —Acts 19:9

Believers can be stubborn and set in their ways, questioning anything new or different that God may want to do in our midst. It was also a common issue during the ministry of Jesus, and it remains so today. The religious people were, and are, the ones most intimidated by His power and threatened by His message. As Josh McDowell and other leaders have said, the last refrain from the lips of believers at the return of Jesus may well be, "We never did it that way before."

The Kingdom Brings Change

Human beings are so afraid of change, yet change is an integral part of the message of our Creator. Beautiful songs and testimonies about change have been written. Thousands of books explaining how to deal with change line the shelves of our libraries and bookstores. More importantly, the written and recorded Word of God speaks of change as an integral part of the plan of God for humanity.

When I think about times of great change in my life, I can remember two significant reactions:

1. Whenever I have reacted negatively to change has been because of fear—specifically the fear of the unknown. One example was when I went to Vietnam. I knew I was flying half a world away to a war zone in the tropical jungles of Asia. I imagined having to run from the aircraft into the bunker amidst a hail of gunfire upon arrival. I had read and watched the news of the airfields being mortared and aircraft receiving gunfire upon approach and departure. Reality was much different. It was uneventful, much like landing anywhere in the U.S. My expectation, colored by my fear, was nothing like what really happened. When I have reacted negatively to change, without exception is when I have allowed the lies and evil imaginations that are brought to me by Satan to remain in my mind while I consider or meditate on them.
2. Whenever I have reacted positively to change has been when I bring whatever is changing in my situations, circumstances, and relationships into

agreement in my mind with what God—and not my situation—has said about me. I have found that it is always about me and my relationship with Him. When I am in relationship with Him, I hear from Him clearly and know exactly what I am supposed to do. I have peace. Hearing is never a problem if I am in that relationship—which, as we have seen, requires fellowship, and commitment to spending time together. God often leads us to take actions that are contrary to the conventional wisdom of the day.

Out of Our Comfort Zone

Earlier in this chapter, I alluded to another major "kingdom move" that God made in my life and Fran's life. Once Fran opened that first jewelry store and I launched the insurance business, things accelerated for us on many fronts. We were thriving in business as we raised our two sons, and we had sunk deep roots in southwestern Georgia. Thomasville was home, and we were building a wonderful life there.

Have you ever noticed, though, that when we are moving in His Spirit and attempting to live as fully as possible as kingdom citizens, there is a certain word that God does not like? The word I am talking about is *comfortable*. Just when we start to feel comfortable, it seems, God presses us to move—maybe not geographically, but always spiritually—so we do not stagnate in His mission for our lives. His kingdom advances forward, not backward.

About fifteen years into owning the jewelry store business, we had already expanded into additional stores. By that time, I also had the insurance business, which had grown by leaps and bounds. Then, another opportunity presented itself in the middle of all this. We had a friend in real estate whom we met during the years that we were restoring the historical home we lived in at the time. It was a large, stately home, and we had just finished a major restoration of the entire property. The last thing we needed was another restoration project (or so I thought).

One day, while I was out of town, the realtor told Fran she had a property she wanted to show her. Fran begged off, but the agent was persistent. Finally, Fran agreed and went to tour what was a large plantation property on the edge of town. The main house had never been out of the original family's ownership; the principal owner had passed away after which it passed to her daughters.

Fran looked at the property and thought it was a fantastic opportunity, even though it needed extensive work. But she knew she could tackle it and get it done, and I had no doubt that she could. When I got back to town, we toured the property with the realtor, then we began to pray about whether we should buy it.

We learned that two sisters owned the property. One sister owned the 18,000-square-foot main house, and the other owned the 10,000-square-foot hunting lodge. Their combined property was over forty acres. A renowned plastic surgeon and his wife had purchased a portion of the expansive property from the sisters, which included approximately forty buildings listed on the National Historic Register, including a theatre where the first screening of "*Gone with the Wind*" was held.

The portion of the property where the hunting lodge sat included a historic brick building that housed a Junior Olympic-sized pool, other historically significant structures, and additional acres. After praying about it, we sensed a green light to move forward, so we bought the sisters' part of the plantation. After extensive renovations, we eventually moved into the 10,000-plus-square-foot hunting lodge known as the Owl's Nest. That was supposed to be it. We were not looking to purchase anything else.

Eventually, however, we became close friends with the plastic surgeon and his wife. They were owners of a plastic surgery clinic as well as the rest of the plantation and acreage. When we were restoring our portion of the property, they would drop in and check on our progress. They were very supportive and offered insights on the history of the plantation—built in 1825 and expanded extensively over the next 150 years.

One day, the surgeon stopped by and said to me, "Charlie, I want to talk to you," with a look on his face that showed this was more than a neighborly visit. He said, "I want to sell you our piece of this property."

I responded, "What in the world would I ever do with forty buildings?" His announcement really caught me off guard, as the idea was not even remotely on my mind or in my plans.

Fran and I began praying about the opportunity, really pressing into God about whether this was something He wanted us to pursue. Up to this time, we had bought the jewelry store with no money, we started the insurance company with no money, but this was something completely different. Operating purely in the world economic system, we understood that we would need to secure a loan to purchase and develop such a large property.

A short period of time passed, and our surgeon friend called from North Carolina, where they owned another farm. They were in the process of moving and invited us to spend the weekend with them to discuss the possibilities of our obtaining their portion of the plantation. As I prayed about our upcoming meeting, I wrote up two different proposals. One was a decent proposal that would work, and the second was the one we felt the property was truly worth (which was less than the first proposal). We were embarrassed to show them the second proposal, not because it was not fair and reasonable, but because we did not want to offend or insult them. We really loved and admired this couple and wanted our business relationship to be a win for them, too. It was an awkward situation.

I was very nervous when Fran and I arrived in North Carolina. The couple gave us a tour of their farm. As I walked, I prayed, "Lord, what am I going do? Which proposal do I give them? I do not want to hurt or offend them." At one point during the night, I even thought about getting in our car and going back home. We would just leave a note thanking them for their invitation but explaining that we had to return quickly to Thomasville. I do not think I slept at all that night.

The next morning, they served a great breakfast and, finally, it was time to talk about the property. They said, "We would really like to know what you are thinking." That was when I gave them the more realistic offer (the second one) and explained that after careful analysis, thought, and prayer, this is what we thought was a fair price and agreement.

Our friend said, "Charlie, that's not at all what we had in mind."

And I thought to myself, "*Okay, Charlie, here is your out. Now, you do not have to do this.*"

He continued, however, and said, "It's really my wife's decision. The property is her baby, and she's the one who has poured herself into it." He proceeded to get up and walk out of the room.

We chatted with his wife for a while and, finally, after about fifteen minutes, she said, "I know that my husband believes you are supposed to have our property, and that this is supposed to be your project." She paused and looked at us. "So—I am going to accept your offer."

Her husband returned shortly with two bags in his hands that were full of keys. He handed me the keys and said, "These are the keys to the forty buildings on the property. There are three rental properties as well. I am going to write to the renters today, tell them that it's yours and to make all payments to you."

Yet again, God caught Fran and me completely off guard. Once I recovered from the shock, I took the bags of keys and mumbled something like, "Wow. Okay, really?"

He said, "We have to have the contracts drawn up, and that's going to take some time. But we know that the property should be yours. We trust you and believe you are people of integrity."

Again—the opportunity of integrity.

Shortly after, we left to make the several-hour drive back home. I do not think I saw anything around us, not a single traffic light all the way home. Fran and I were in shock, but we also knew that only God could have orchestrated something so unlikely and amazing.

This was a defining moment in my understanding of the principle of eternality and the reality of God's operating system—His kingdom dynamics and systems. Even though I did not fully realize it in the moment, looking back now, I clearly see the "leap" I made that day when our friends said yes to our offer.

Though we had been praying earnestly about the possibility of buying their part of the property, we were not fully prepared for the outcome. We believed it would take time—months of negotiations and agreements. The entire scene with our friends that morning had been dripping with scriptural analogy. We were handed the keys—with no money down and no signed contract. Just our word.

The situation was a case of "be careful what you wish (or pray) for." But here is the important conclusion: when you decide to follow Jesus, He will open an unexpected door and you will say, "Wait, you want me to do what? I am not sure I am ready for this." That is what happens when you are walking in His kingdom. Fran and I were functioning in kingdom dynamics and, at the time, we did not realize what that meant.

The everyday world—in the kingdom of darkness—is not based on the principle of eternality. Far from it. It is based in things that are temporal (the view that all we have is right now and that we need to grab for the brass ring, "get what is ours," and "the ends justify the means" even if it means cheating and stealing). Fran and I would soon find out that this type of earthly faith view is how many Christian businesspeople operate as well.

Before our trip to North Carolina, I thought for sure that once we discussed an offer, our friends would want to think about the offer for a while. I assumed they would draw up contracts and that negotiations would take several more months. I told Fran that it would be six months, at the earliest if they accepted our offer, before we would take ownership.

Yet, here we were, back in Thomasville the next day with the keys to all of their buildings. Like the first jewelry store and the insurance business, here we were again, taking possession of this amazing property without having to pay any money. Only God can open doors like that, and it would not have happened if we were not walking in His kingdom principles and dynamics.

Suddenly, my "six-month timeline" had shrunk down to a couple of days! Of course, to finance something this large, we needed to acquire funding from the bank. So I set up an appointment with a friend at our bank, and we were approved for a loan. From there, we started to renovate the buildings and create a plan for the opening of a business.

Our surgeon friend called me and said, "I am going to do you a huge favor and introduce you to a gentleman who has been doing all my renovations over the years. He's a master—all you need to do is tell him what you want or draw a little sketch, and he's a genius at making it happen."

I was a little skeptical, but my friend was correct. This builder named Ken became our right-hand man and trusted confidant throughout the entire multi-year process of getting the property renovated and reconstructed to a high level of restoration. When renovating any of the forty buildings, we would walk into our meeting with a piece of paper or cardboard, and stand with Ken while sketching what we wanted the project to become. Then he would build it. He truly was a genius.

Then, the very hard work began. We set about renovating the entire property, then developing the business into a luxury plantation resort. As we prayed and planned the vision for the plantation, the Lord gave us a picture of a castle (or a version of an American castle). While we do not have castles in the US, the closest thing to it could be a plantation. We went to work on the restoration with absolute dedication and fervor. Sometimes, we worked eighteen-hour days to get the property ready to open as a historical southern plantation resort with a fine-dining restaurant.

The main house had eleven guest suites, and the property totaled thirty-nine guest rooms. We focused on hiring and training staff as well as opening the fine-dining restaurant. Once open, we brought in chefs from all over the world, including South Africa, France, and Argentina.

We trained our hospitality team according to the principles we see in God's Word because we wanted our future guests to experience true Southern hospitality in a refined atmosphere.

Though this book is not large enough to share all the details of our journey in renovating and opening the resort, the process was arduous and back-breaking but exhilarating.

Opening day was set for January 1998. We were not finished with all the rooms by that day, so as guests were arriving through the front door, the workers and decorators were going out the back door. We worked until ten or eleven o'clock and were up at four-thirty in the morning to get everything ready for opening day. We opened our doors having completed what was referred to as the prominent plantation home; however, that was only a small portion of the entire property. We kept working on the project, renovating each building, and upon completion, opening each facility to the public.

Immediately after we opened, God gave us enormous favor. Word of our property spread very quickly, and soon we had guests arriving from around the world—more than thirty countries. In fact, one summer we had more international guests than guests from the U.S. Celebrities also made up our guest list, and journalists and other members of the media flew in for pictures, interviews, and articles about the plantation resort. In all, I believe we have had more than 5,000 articles written about the historic plantation and its amenities. We became a Relais & Chateaux property (a very prestigious hospitality organization), of which there are only about 400 across the globe.

Over the next two years, we continued to renovate additional historic buildings—one by one, room by room. Our goal was to carefully restore the entire plantation without damaging its historic value or character.

Oftentimes, Fran would be asked, "How did you make this happen? It is absolutely amazing; how you have recreated a place that captures the grandeur of the old South? Was this your dream?" And Fran would say, "Heck no, it was not one of my dreams. This is the hardest work I have ever done."

The key word in the entire process of obtaining and renovating the plantation was "kingdom." This process was when Fran and I began to truly learn about kingdom dynamics and what it means to fully walk in God's kingdom. It is how we have lived for, now, more than twenty-five years.

Fast forward to September 11, 2001. We were close to finishing all renovations and restorations, then 9/11 happened, and no one could travel anywhere, all over the world. The entire property was leased to a family from Ireland for a wedding, followed by numerous other large parties that were scheduled for the following months. But of course, the Irish family could not travel, and they had paid a significant deposit. We knew God would not have us keep their money. So over the next two years, we sent back more money to future guests than we were taking in. Could we have pocketed some, or all, the money from cancellations? Yes. But that would not be a kingdom move; we would not have stayed within the guidelines and dynamics of the Kingdom System.

God had opened miraculous doors that had put us in this position, and we were having enormous success. In the final days of completion of the renovation, everything started to change. All of a sudden, after 9/11, it was like the once open doors closed. Of course, we had taken out construction loans to complete different phases—that is how this type of large project works. We had completed all phases, as agreed, and were prepared for a timely finish. Things were intense.

We were about ninety days from finishing our two-year renovation project. I called our banker—the one who had secured our initial loan—and gave him a progress report on the renovations and explained that we were going to finish a little early. He told me he would get back to me, but he never did.

I found out the bank had been bought by a bigger bank originating from Florida. My banker friend who had given me the initial construction loan said, "Charlie, I need to talk to you. You and I need to get some paperwork done pretty quickly." We were supposed to connect on a particular date, but that day came and went, and he was unreachable at his workplace.

Finally, I reached him at home on his cell phone and he said, "Charlie, I am not there anymore. They fired me, and I am telling you, you need to watch your back because they are coming after you." And I thought, *Lord, why would they want to do that?* We had been making our loan payments on time, and we were very close to the completion of the project and the arrangement of our permanent financing. It did not make sense.

What happened next was something you just cannot make up. Only God could have arranged it. How we learned of what was truly happening with the new holder of our loan was simply phenomenal. It was a kingdom phenomenon; I am fully convinced.

What the Enemy Meant for Evil, God Meant for Good

Now that my friend had been fired, I reached out to the new person who was managing our loan. Unfortunately, however, he had no authority to work on our behalf. This was two months before the loan note was due for renewal, and I told him we needed to get it renewed. He said he would get the paperwork ready and get back to me, but he never did. I called him, repeatedly, and finally, the day that my note was due, I got a certified letter in the mail. They were calling the note. The new holder of my loan was requiring me to submit payment *in full.* At this point in this development process, we were highly leveraged, and this was not possible.

In the state of Georgia, you have only thirty days to cure a default. Now, as all this was happening, God was at work behind the scenes—as he always is—to make some truly phenomenal kingdom moves that we could not have made in the natural realm. They were truly miraculous moves seated in the realm of eternality—in the flow of His Kingdom System.

The first move God made was through a good friend who was approached by a small investment and banking group. They shared with him their plan to, basically, execute a hostile takeover of the plantation and our business. Our friend said, "I'm not going be a part of this because I'm friends with Charlie and Fran." When these investors pushed him, he warned them. He said, "You do not know what you are dealing with. If you pursue this—which I highly recommend you do not—you will find out that you cannot take it from Charlie and his family.

Our friend's words became prophetic, as you will see.

Here is the next kingdom move that only God would orchestrate: since opening the plantation property, we had become friends with the man who was the Commissioner of Industry, Tourism, and Trade for the state of Georgia. He loved what we were doing and wanted our place to be a destination in the southwest region of Georgia. He was working with us to promote the greater Thomasville area for industry, tourism, and trade.

Thomasville has rich historical roots, and there is enough history here to make it a major destination. So the commissioner visited the plantation several times and spent the night in our property. He was a wonderful man, and we had an excellent working relationship.

During the tumultuous time when the bank had called our note, the commissioner came down for a visit, then left our place to attend a fundraising banquet for the state of Georgia in the beautiful beach community of St. Simons. At about eleven o'clock one night, my phone rang, and it was the Commissioner. He asked what I was doing, and I told him I was just about to go to bed.

"No, tell me what's going on there with you," he said.

"I do not know what you mean," I said. He then proceeded to tell me an incredible "only-God" type of story. It turns out that at this fundraising dinner for the Governor, the Tourism Commissioner was seated at the same table as a man who was a major leader in the Georgia Chamber of Commerce. He lived in Thomasville but was from a blue blood family with many connections across the state. This man from the Chamber of Commerce snubbed the Commissioner and treated him disrespectfully because he did not know who he was.

Everyone who entered the banquet that evening, however, made their way over to the Commissioner to greet him and talk with him, including the governor. Now, suddenly, this rude gentleman is curious and thinking, "*Who is this guy?*" And he said to our friend, "Now tell me again who you are?"

"I am the Commissioner of Industry, Tourism, and Trade for the state of Georgia."

"Well, I need to know you; you need to come to Thomasville," the man said.

"I've been to Thomasville four times in the last month and a half," said the Commissioner.

"You've been to Thomasville, and you haven't come to see me?"

"No. I've been to see Charlie and Fran Lewis four times. And if I go back, that's who I am going to see, and that is who I will be staying with."

The Commissioner made it obvious that he was calling out the leader from the Chamber. Here is the most amazing part: the chamber leader proceeded to tell the Commissioner that he is part of a group of investors that had come together and bought our note after the bank had been purchased. In short, they were trying to take our business and our property. This group knew that post-9/11 was a brutal time for hospitality, and they thought they would take advantage of the situation and push us out.

Of course, by the time the Commissioner and I ended our phone call, all the pieces started to come together for me. It was a moment of kingdom revelation in that God miraculously allowed our friend, the Commissioner, to be seated at the same table as this member of the hostile takeover group. Coincidence? No. What's more, this chamber leader proceeded to do something that experienced businesspeople just do not do: share highly sensitive and confidential information around a banquet table—and with our ally!

This bit of information allowed Fran, me, and my family to pray proactively and fervently against the defeated Satan's moves against our business. We went from a position of not knowing nor understanding to a position of knowledge and discernment, which allowed us to go on the spiritual offensive.

The next few months were some of the most stressful of our lives. I would be awake often until the early hours of the morning seeking God's direction and praying for His favor and His kingdom plans for me and our family. I can honestly say that, at times, I was experiencing terror. This was the most intense "kingdom schooling" I had been through, to date, because I needed to learn these concepts and dynamics, right now.

What came next was another set of miracles. Remember, I don't use the word supernatural, because it sounds like God's moves in the realm of eternality are not the norm. What I discovered during this very stressful season is that when you have completely surrendered to His kingdom and His dynamics of being and doing good, He breaks into the normal and delivers the miraculous. That is eternality in action—seeing eternal direction and outcome. That is what the kingdom of God looks like daily when you are moving and operating according to the dynamics of His operating system.

In the midst of this hellish storm, I was sitting quietly and praying at my desk. I said, "Lord, I don't understand why this is happening. No one can do this to me unless You allow them to. And You would not allow them to unless there is something You want me to know and to understand. You said if I don't know I can ask, and You will tell me. So, God, this is me asking You: what is it?"

The Holy Spirit said, "I want you to go to the New Testament, and I want you to read everything that I said when I was on the earth."

I was so busy that the directive annoyed me. I said, "Yeah, I know, all the stuff in red."

"Yes, I want you to read it all."

Because my life was so hectic, it took me several weeks to do. But, at the end of reading all the words of Jesus—the red-letter words—I still did not have a clue as to what God was trying to show me. I said, "Okay, Lord, I have read it."

God responded, and in my spirit, He said, "No, you haven't Charlie."

I was not happy. I said, "Now, Lord, that bothers me." It made me really upset because I had carefully and prayerfully read exactly what He told me to read.

"No, Charlie, you read it with your religious mind. You didn't read it with an open spirit to hear what my Spirit wants to say to your spirit."

I had read Watchman Nee's classic *The Spiritual Man*, and I understood spirit, mind, and body. I realized that I had read it with my intellect, not through a lens of eternality—not with my spirit. I said, "Lord, I repent, and I ask you to forgive me. I will read it again, with an open spirit."

I took the next couple of months to re-read everything I had already read, but this time I allowed the red letters to reach my spirit.

God asked me, "What do you think?"

I said, "Lord, I don't know a bit more about what you want me to know than before I read it."

He asked me another question, "What did you get out of it?"

That is when the paradigm shift started to occur, and I began to see the material through an eternal lens. I said, "When you were on the earth in the person of Jesus Christ, you didn't teach any of the things that I've been taught in church. You didn't teach the stuff that has become so important in faith today to the church."

He said, "No, what did I teach?"

I said, "You taught the kingdom of God. That is basically all you taught. That was the central theme and the primary message You delivered when You were on the earth—the kingdom of God.

God said, "That's right. You have it."

That was the major turning point. That is when eternality became a clearer reality to me; that is when the things I had been walking in—without even knowing it—became conscious to my spirit. It was when reality of His Kingdom System became more than a concept or an intellectual premise—it became reality.

My breakthrough didn't make all my problems suddenly disappear, but it was the beginning of the end for many of them. To my amazement, a series of delays began to take place. To explain, each time the hostile banking group set a deadline for forfeiture of the note and the property, the deadline would pass without incident. This happened *repeatedly* over a nine-month period.

At one point, we were taken to court. To shorten what is otherwise a very long story, the court case was just as miraculous as the other series of events I have already shared with you. Things looked bleak in court. I was deeply berated by the opposition composed mostly of government attorneys.

Then, one of the attorneys for the opposing side stood up and defended me and my character. He said, "We have known Mr. Lewis for years now, and everything he has told us has been true. Our counsel has talked, and we would like to give him the opportunity to perform what he believes his plan will produce. We believe that he will be successful."

Another opportunity of integrity!

It infuriated the other opposing attorneys. This gentleman went out of his way to say that I had done nothing wrong and that the case should be thrown out.

It finally was!

In the end, the plot of these investors failed. And though it was a long, hard fight over several years, we prevailed. From the world's perspective, there is no way our family should have survived this assault. This investor group had very deep pockets, a team of expensive attorneys, and were ready and able to outspend and outlast our family; however, against all odds, God saw us through. This process was how Fran and I began to fully understand the power and purpose of God's kingdom on Earth as it is in heaven.

You really do not want to go against God and His kingdom plans. That is not me boasting in myself or in my talents. That is me boasting in the kingdom of God and the perfect symmetry and order of His eternal Kingdom System. What the enemy meant for evil, God meant for good. The entire scheme was straight from the kingdom of darkness. But God exposed it through a mutual friend who "just happened" to be seated at the same table at a banquet as one of the instigators of this plan to destroy our business, investments, and family.

Coincidence? There are no coincidences in God's kingdom. In fact as stated previously, there is no Hebrew word for coincidence. His ways are always purposeful, and as we submit ourselves to His rich principles and precepts, He will be faithful to guide us through. Will it be in the way we perceive or conceive it? Usually not, because we only see in part; He sees the whole. We see a little, but He sees the complete picture through to the finish. Eternality.

Are You Ready for Change?

Imagine someone asking you, "Have you received the kingdom since you believed?" How would you answer? Perhaps your response would be, "I have not heard of the kingdom," or "I have made it this far without understanding the kingdom," or "Wow, how exciting!" I hope you are excited about God's invitation to step into His way of doing things correctly and live as a kingdom citizen as fully as you can.

We do not need to be afraid of the changes a kingdom lifestyle brings or the power that is found in the understanding. Our Father God is not playing tricks on us. He is not holding promises in front of us, just out of our reach. He is excited about our discovering His plan and His system so we can live as He instructed—in power and dominion and authority.

This kingdom is the redemptive system of governance and the power and the authority that God Himself as Jesus of Nazareth delivered to Earth for humanity. This Kingdom System is given to us so we can operate in His power, in His dynamics, and in His principles. This kingdom gives us the power, the authority, and the dominion to bring heaven to Earth to impact the outcomes of human lives. The experience and the blessing are available now.

If this kingdom lifestyle makes you nervous or intimidates you, listen to what Jesus said about those who will follow Him:

> *Are you tired? Worn out? Burned out on religion? Come to me. Get away with me and you'll recover your life. I'll show you how to take a real rest. Walk with me and work with me—watch how I do it. Learn the unforced rhythms of grace. I won't lay anything heavy or ill-fitting on you. Keep company with me and you'll learn to live freely and lightly.*
>
> —Matthew 11:28-30, MSG

In this kingdom, fear is defeated. More than 365 times, the Scriptures say not to be afraid or not to fear. No matter the situations, the circumstances, and the relationships, we know the outcome from the beginning. The outcome is not related to the situation but to our relationship with the King. No matter the result of the trial, what the doctor says, what the bank says, what the attorneys declare to be true, or what our checkbook reflects, we do not have to walk in fear.

We understand that whatever the defeated Satan and the forces of the kingdom of darkness do to kill, steal, or destroy us, our God will turn all of it into good for us if we believe Him, accept what He says, write and cash the check of faith (Romans 8:28). In every situation, we are made to triumph through Christ Jesus (2 Corinthians 2:14).

We must accept and believe what our God says about us. We must confess with our mouths His truth. There can be no looking back, no matter how big the giant, how tall the mountain, or how many our foes. The government and the governance system of heaven's realm provided by our God rules over everything and reigns supreme.

Be open and receptive to what God brings into your life. Allow Him and His Word to change the way you think. Accept and receive the reality of the kingdom of God, both in relationship and in benefit.

Choose His Government

Most Christians claim faith in God but do not understand how to live under His kingdom government and His governance. Instead, they have put their faith in the ways and the governments of the earth. We do not know, nor do we understand, how to utilize our faith in the kingdom government of God. We appear not to need the provisions of His government or to seem unaware that they exist. We engage with the governments and with the systems of this world, substituting their provision for the provision found in the kingdom government of our God. We will not experience overcoming victory anywhere but in following His redemptive governance plan.

Too often, the church has not taught us about the kingdom government of our God. We do not know that it is available or even what it is. The Word is filtered through lenses of temporality and earthly laws and rules rather than eternality and the dynamics and systems of His forever kingdom. As a result, we struggle to utilize the innate power and provision delivered to humanity by Jesus.

God did not come to Earth, and suffer unimaginable physical and emotional pain, to provide a way for us to walk in victory simply so we could live in misery and at the whims of a defeated Satan. We must be witnesses and display for all to see what the kingdom government of God is and what it does. He gave us this government system so we could operate on Earth to fulfill the dominion mandate He assigned to us. In coming to Earth as the Holy Spirit God to reside inside of us, He provided the ability to have constant direction and powerful influence in every situation, circumstance, and relationship.

How do we live in eternality *right now*—where we live every moment of every day in that system and walk in the victory offered by God through His kingdom? We invite the Holy Spirit God to enter our spirit and to dwell there. We study the provided instructions—our Constitution, God's Word—and we apply the dynamics, the values, the principles, and the established precedents in our daily lives with every breath we take.

Dynamics and values are not optional. If we are to walk in His plan and experience His provision, we are to know and to understand His instructions to then follow them to the letter. They are not difficult or too onerous to bear. They are a pleasure to know and to understand. They are His expression of love for us, His people. They are for our good. And they work.

We must exercise our faith in our knowledge of the kingdom government and the redemptive governance plan of our God. Muscles are not developed instantly or overnight. We must use the faith and the understanding we have. By that exercise, our kingdom government muscles will grow. We will become strong and powerful in the knowledge and power of the kingdom governance of our God.

Why is this important? You can only get from a storehouse what has already been placed inside of it by the owner of the storehouse. *If the storehouse you seek to draw from is in the possession of the government of the world, you will only be able to extract from it the things of the world—whether those things are material, intellectual, spiritual, or anything else.*

Too often when we experience being born again, we are told about redemption but not about restoration. So we continue to conduct our lives and our business by the laws and principles of the world. We experience defeat and frustration mentally, emotionally, physically, financially, relationally, and spiritually—not because there is no plan for victory; but because we do not seek, strive after, long for, and hunger ravenously for His kingdom, His government, His plan, its governance, and His way of doing and being right.

We have become and are now citizens of a nation whose author and founder is Jesus Christ. We cannot afford to walk away from His provision and look to the provision of the world. We must learn about His plan, His provision, and His governance. We must seek it with everything we have—every ounce of our energy. Then others will see and know there is only one God, the True and the Living God. He has provided very well for His citizens.

In Matthew 25:14-30, Jesus told a parable of a master going away and leaving various amounts of his money with three of his servants for them to invest. Two of the servants multiplied what the master had given, while one buried the money given to him to protect it. The master commended those who took risks and multiplied their investments, but he had harsh words for the one who simply tried to hold on to what he had been given. We can make some interesting observations from this parable.

1. It is not the amount of the gift but the return or increase on the gift that matters.
2. God is concerned with the results of our efforts.
3. God gives us gifts according to our abilities.
4. God calls increase "good" and declares us to be faithful. He invites us to celebrate with Him and says we will receive more because of our results.
5. God sees a lack of growth as "bad" and declares us to be unfaithful, even wicked, if we fail to have growth. The servant without any increase was banned to outer darkness where there is weeping and gnashing of teeth. That is not a place any of us would want to visit.

6. The master took the unfaithful servant's only talent away and gave it to the servant with the most talents, and Jesus said this is the way of the kingdom.
7. God redistributes His resources—spiritual, physical, vocational, and economic resources—to those who can multiply what He has given. Jesus said, "To those who use well what they are given, even more will be given, and they will have an abundance. But from those who do nothing, even what little they have will be taken away" (Matthew 25:29).

We must use the gifts God has given us, and He will bless them and multiply them tremendously, no matter the size of the gift. He is the God of multiplication and increase. If we are not experiencing growth, no matter what the trends of the world are doing, we may not be operating in the true and correct kingdom that God has given us.

God gives each of us gifts. Everyone has at least one. While Joseph was in slavery and even in prison, he prospered and profited every time he was given the opportunity to operate in the gift God had given him. His circumstances were not good, and the world around him was in turmoil. Still, this did not prevent him from prospering.

The attitude of entitlement that is found everywhere today is in direct opposition to God's ways. We do not receive from God and His kingdom because we deserve it, but because we follow His plan. His plan declares that when we obey His commandments, we can and are instructed to ask, to seek, and to knock (Matthew 7:7-8). Our belief is that the results He promised are there now, no matter the circumstances, the situations, or the relationships. When we declare with our mouths that His Word and His promises are true, faith rises, and the results follow.

I have a friend who likes to say that the blessing or the miracle is in the motion. God is not motivated by need but by seed. We must plant a seed to receive. No matter how big the seed or the gift, it is God who gives the increase. In His kingdom, we hold the understanding of the most powerful method of operating and living, successfully, on the earth. The absolute unfailing method of obtaining wholeness, peace, wellbeing, health, wealth, power, and success in every area of our lives is in understanding and using His kingdom operating system.

See and understand what God has put into your hands now. Take the gifts He has given you and sow them as seeds in His kingdom of promise. Learn the ways of His kingdom government and governance. Be faithful, consistent, and persistent. What you have sown will grow without fail. Jesus said that if we are faithful over little things, He will make us rulers over great things.

Pursue, Overtake, and Recover All

Before David became king of Israel, he and his band of warriors returned to their home base in a town called Ziklag only to find that it had been raided (1 Samuel 30). Enemy Amalekites had come into the town, burned it down, and taken all the women and children of David and his men. It was a devastating attack, and the men began to turn against David. The blessings God had given them had been stolen.

David "strengthened himself in the Lord" and was able to regain his composure enough to ask God for direction. Should he pursue the raiders and battle them? Yes, God said. David overtook them and recovered what was taken. God promised him victory.

This is a dramatic picture of our kingdom mission. God was teaching David a lesson on how to be king over Israel, but in this story He also teaches us a valuable lesson on how to rule as His children in His kingdom. We must protect what we have been given as well as recover what the enemy has taken from us.

Before David could be an effective ruler over God's people, he had to learn how to protect his investments—the things God had already given him. Too often, we try to advance God's cause without properly protecting our anointing, our heart, our families, and our possessions. God has given each of us stewardship over what we currently have, and He wants to see how we handle it.

In Jesus' parable of the talents, the master said to one of the faithful servants, "Well done, my good and faithful servant. You have been faithful in handling this small amount, so now I will give you many more responsibilities. Let's celebrate together!" (Matthew 25:23). How we handle the blessings God has given us is a big issue in His kingdom.

In ancient warfare, when a king went out to battle, he never sent all his resources out of the city to advance his kingdom. He always left skilled fighters behind so the enemy would not overthrow him. If the enemy knew a king was leaving town without protecting the fortified city, he would simply wait for the king to leave and then go plunder without any resistance.

This was a hard lesson for David to learn, but I am sure it is one he never forgot. He never again left unprotected what God had given him. Often people try to save the world without regard to their own families. It is easy to get sidetracked while trying to do too much outside of our own house. We must make sure our house is in order before we try to save someone else.

The lesson in this story is not only that we should protect what God has given us. As kingdom citizens, we also must learn to recover what has been lost or stolen. This is what we are doing when we bring heaven to bear in our situations, circumstances, and relationships on earth. David asked God if he should go up and pursue the raiders. Would he be successful? Would he overtake them? God answered, "Pursue." He assured David that he would overtake the raiders and recover all.

David had just suffered a devastating loss, but he encouraged himself enough to ask God what to do. God may allow you to lose a battle here and there, but if you follow His plans, you will not lose the war. In Christ, the battle has already been fought for the kingdom and its citizens. God has given us complete victory over the enemy. Our job is to renew our mind so we begin to think like God thinks and to walk in eternality. God wants us to recover what has been stolen; Jesus came to establish the kingdom of God, recover all that was lost, and destroy all the works of the defeated Satan. If God told us to recover all, then we ought to have the mindset to do just that and nothing less.

According to Luke 19:10, this was Jesus' mission—the Son of Man came to seek and save what was lost—and it is our mission, too. Jesus sends us out to have dominion in this world and to bring the kingdom of heaven to Earth.

People sometimes think that there is shame in being "in recovery." The truth of the matter is that we should all be, or have already been, in recovery. At different times in our walk with God, we will recognize that the defeated Satan stole something from us, and we must recover it. Maybe your quiet time that you used to spend with God has diminished. You may be lacking when it comes to reading the Word, or your zeal for God's house that once consumed you has now been reduced to smoldering ash.

Maybe you have suffered losses in your health, your relationships, or your finances. Perhaps you have been pushed around by the enemy and suffered injustices that were not God's good will for you. Whatever you find lacking, do not ever be ashamed to go into recovery mode. Do not let the enemy fool you into staying on your feet. Get down on your knees and inquire of the Lord.

David pursued what was rightfully his, and that is the attitude we should take. Peace belongs to us! Joy belongs to us! All the blessings of God belong to us! Jesus said it is God's good pleasure to give us the kingdom, so let's take authority like David did. David and his men took off after the enemy.

Some went all the way, while others were exhausted and lagged to guard the equipment. Still, they were all one. God's people should always advance as one, no matter what job they are doing. If they are doing it for God, everyone in the family of God should enjoy the same spoils. The kingdom belongs to all of God's children.

As citizens of the kingdom of God who live with a kingdom mindset and under the government of the King, we are to bring the government of heaven to Earth. In this book, we have talked a lot about the attitudes, actions, and words you will need to do this. Remember that this is not just a destination, it is a journey. You cannot just say one day, "I am in the kingdom, so all this is manifested for me." You choose to live in the kingdom and by its dynamics and principles, and then you set out to create the culture around you that allows the kingdom to operate freely and effectively.

That means that when darkness presents itself, you interject light into it. You compare what the kingdom of darkness is doing and saying to what the kingdom of light says, and you choose to fill your spirit and mind with truth and light. When people tell you that you cannot win the battle against darkness, you tell them that God says we overcome by our faith.

You take God's two-edged sword, His Word, and stand on it. You resolutely refuse to bow to any other thought or idea that does not fit with what He has said and promised. When the darkness comes against you—and it will if you are living as a kingdom citizen—you choose to live only by the light. You refuse to be deceived.

Remember that you cannot press a button and make this happen. It is a relationship with God. In that context, you learn His thoughts, plans, and purposes and align yourself with them. As you do, you will find the kingdom coming in your life and in the world around you.

YOUR DECLARATIONS

YOU HAVE GOD'S FAVOR

Our God has generously provided all we need. We always have everything we need, and there is always plenty left over to share with others (2 Corinthians 9:8).

Through Your favor Lord, you caused the Egyptians to look favorably on the Israelites, and they gave the Israelites whatever they asked for. They plundered the Egyptians of their wealth. God, You are the same today; You do not change (Exodus 12:36).

Lord, You were with Joseph in the prison; You showed him Your faithful love and also made him a favorite with the prison warden (Genesis 39:21). In every situation we are made to triumph through Christ Jesus.

Lord, You declared that when we are obedient we grow in wisdom and in stature and in favor with You, God and with the people (Luke 2:52). Thank you because Your face shines upon us.

Lord, Your people did not conquer the land with their swords; it was not their own strong arm that gave them victory. It was Your right hand, Your strong arm, and the blinding light from Your face that helped them because You loved them (Psalm 44:3). They were set apart as we, your people, are set apart today for You. Thank You Father that we are called and we are designed according to Your purpose.

Lord, may You arise and have mercy on Zion. The time to favor her, yes, the set time, has come (Psalm 102:13). We receive your favor. We are strong and do exploits through our God.

All of the declarations found here, and many more, are available in the book Kingdom Activating Declarations by Charlie Lewis.

Visit www.ksam.net for this and other great resources.

YOUR DECLARATIONS

GOD'S FAVOR DECLARED AND ENGAGED

Father God, list your name and your family members' names here, and all of your heirs and all of your descendants forever: we declare that we receive and we live in Your favor in our lives today. We are Your righteousness; we are recipients of your covenant kindness and Your covenant favor. We thank You because Your favor surrounds us like a shield everywhere we go, in everything we do, and with everyone we meet. We expect good things to manifest in our lives today and every day because Your divine favor is upon us. Your favor in our lives is immeasurable, unlimited, and lavishly abounds toward us.

Father, we are grateful to You that Your special favor produces miraculous increase, promotion, restoration, honor, increased assets, greater victories, prominence, recognition, preferential treatment, petitions granted, policies and rules changed, and battles won in which we do not have to fight. The spotlight of Your favor is on our lives now. Thank You for causing Your face to shine upon us and for giving us an abundance of favor with You and with man.

This is our year of favor, and our lives are full of you favor, in Jesus' name. Amen.

All of the declarations found here, and many more, are available in the book Kingdom Activating Declarations by Charlie Lewis.

Visit www.ksam.net for this and other great resources.

APPENDIX

Scripture contains numerous statements that demonstrate a conditional *if-then* dynamic between God and His people. The following verses, quoted are from the New International Version (2011), represent a sample of them.

> "If you obey me fully and keep my covenant, then out of all nations you will be my treasured possession. Although the whole earth is mine, you will be for me a kingdom of priests and a holy nation." (Exodus 19:5-6)

> "If you listen carefully to what he says and do all that I say, I will be an enemy to your enemies and will oppose those who oppose you." (Exodus 23:22)

> "If you pay attention to these laws and are careful to follow them, then the Lord your God will keep his covenant of love with you, as he swore to your ancestors. He will love you and bless you and increase your numbers." (Deuteronomy 7:12-13)

> "If you fully obey the Lord your God and carefully follow all his commands I give you today, the Lord your God will

set you high above all the nations on earth. All these blessings will come on you and accompany you if you obey the Lord your God." (Deuteronomy 28:1-2)

"If you do not obey the Lord your God and do not carefully follow all his commands and decrees I am giving you today, all these curses will come on you and overtake you." (Deuteronomy 28:15)

"The Lord will again delight in you and make you prosperous, just as he delighted in your ancestors, if you obey the Lord your God and keep his commands and decrees that are written in this Book of the Law and turn to the Lord your God with all your heart and with all your soul." (Deuteronomy 30:9-10)

"If your heart turns away and you are not obedient, and if you are drawn away to bow down to other gods and worship them, I declare to you this day that you will certainly be destroyed. You will not live long in the land you are crossing the Jordan to enter and possess. This day I call the heavens and the earth as witnesses against you that I have set before you life and death, blessings and curses. Now choose life, so that you and your children may live and that you may love the Lord your God, listen to his voice, and hold fast to him." (Deuteronomy 30:17-20)

"If my people, who are called by my name, will humble themselves and pray and seek my face and turn from their wicked ways, then I will hear from heaven, and I will forgive their sin and will heal their land." (2 Chronicles 7:14)

"If you walk before me faithfully as David your father did, and do all I command, and observe my decrees and laws, I will establish your royal throne, as I covenanted with David your father when I said, 'You shall never fail to have a successor to rule over Israel.'" (2 Chronicles 7:17-18)

"If you turn away and forsake the decrees and commands I have given you and go off to serve other gods and worship them, then I will uproot Israel from my land, which I have given them, and will reject this temple I have consecrated for my Name." (2 Chronicles 7:19)

"If you return to the Lord, then your fellow Israelites and your children will be shown compassion by their captors and will return to this land, for the Lord your God is gracious and compassionate. He will not turn his face from you if you return to him." (2 Chronicles 30:9)

"Remember the instruction you gave your servant Moses, saying, 'If you are unfaithful, I will scatter you among the nations, but if you return to me and obey my commands, then even if your exiled people are at the farthest horizon, I will gather them from there and bring them to the place I have chosen as a dwelling for my Name.'" (Nehemiah 1:8-9)

"If your sons keep my covenant and the statutes I teach them, then their sons will sit on your throne for ever and ever." (Psalm 132:12)

My son, if you receive my words, and treasure my commands within you, so that you incline your ear to wisdom, and apply your heart to understanding; yes, if you cry out for discernment, and lift up your voice for understanding, if you seek her as silver, and search for her as for hidden treasures; then you will understand the fear of the Lord, and find the knowledge of God." (Proverbs 2:1-5)

"If you do away with the yoke of oppression, with the pointing finger and malicious talk, and if you spend yourselves in behalf of the hungry and satisfy the needs of the oppressed, then your light will rise in the darkness, and your night will become like the noonday. The Lord will guide you always; he will satisfy your needs in a sun-scorched land and will strengthen your frame. You will be like a well watered garden, like a spring whose waters never fail. Your people will rebuild the ancient ruins and will raise up the age-old foundations; you will be called Repairer of Broken Walls, Restorer of Streets with Dwellings. "If you keep your feet from breaking the Sabbath and from doing as you please on my holy day, if you call the Sabbath a delight and the Lord's holy day honorable, and if you honor it by not going your own way and not doing as you please or speaking idle words, then you will find your joy in the Lord, and I will cause you to ride in triumph on the heights of the land and to feast on the inheritance of your father Jacob." For the mouth of the Lord has spoken." (Isaiah 58:9-14)

"If they learn well the ways of my people and swear by my name, saying, 'As surely as the Lord lives'—even as they once taught my people to swear by Baal—then they will be established among my people. But if any nation does not listen, I will completely uproot and destroy it," declares the Lord." (Jeremiah 12:16-17)

"If you do not obey me to keep the Sabbath day holy by not carrying any load as you come through the gates of Jerusalem on the Sabbath day, then I will kindle an unquenchable fire in the gates of Jerusalem that will consume her fortresses.'" (Jeremiah 17:27)

"If at any time I announce that a nation or kingdom is to be uprooted, torn down and destroyed, and if that nation I warned repents of its evil, then I will relent and not inflict on it the disaster I had planned. And if at another time I announce that a nation or kingdom is to be built up and planted, and if it does evil in my sight and does not obey me, then I will reconsider the good I had intended to do for it." (Jeremiah 18:7-10)

"If you are careful to carry out these commands, then kings who sit on David's throne will come through the gates of this palace, riding in chariots and on horses, accompanied by their officials and their people. But if you do not obey these commands, declares the Lord, I swear by myself that this palace will become a ruin.'" (Jeremiah 22:4-5)

"You will seek me and find me when you seek me with all your heart." (Jeremiah 29:13)

"This is what the Lord Almighty says: 'If you will walk in obedience to me and keep my requirements, then you will govern my House and have charge of my courts, and I will give you a place among these standing here.'" (Zechariah 3:7)

"Bring the whole tithe into the storehouse, that there may be food in my house. Test me in this," says the Lord Almighty, "and see if I will not throw open the floodgates of heaven and pour out so much blessing that there will not be room enough to store it." (Malachi 3:10)

"Truly I tell you that if two of you on earth agree about anything they ask for, it will be done for them by my Father in heaven. For where two or three gather in my name, there am I with them." (Matthew 18:19-20)

"Truly I tell you, if you have faith and do not doubt, not only can you do what was done to the fig tree, but also you can say to this mountain, 'Go, throw yourself into the sea,' and it will be done. If you believe, you will receive whatever you ask for in prayer." (Matthew 21:21-22)

"So I say to you: ask and it will be given to you; seek and you will find; knock and the door will be opened to you. For everyone who asks receives; the one who seeks finds; and to the one who knocks, the door will be opened." (Luke 11:9-10)

"If you then, though you are evil, know how to give good gifts to your children, how much more will your Father in heaven give the Holy Spirit to those who ask him!" (Luke 11:13)

"If you remain in me and I in you, you will bear much fruit; apart from me you can do nothing. If you do not remain in me, you are like a branch that is thrown away and withers; such branches are picked up, thrown into the fire and burned. If you remain in me and my words remain in you, ask whatever you wish, and it will be done for you." (John 15:5-7)

If we are children, then we are heirs—heirs of God and co-heirs with Christ, if indeed we share in his sufferings in order that we may also share in his glory. (Romans 8:17)

"Here I am! I stand at the door and knock. If anyone hears my voice and opens the door, I will come in and eat with that person, and they with me." (Revelation 3:20)

ENDNOTES

1 James Allen, As A Man Thinketh, (Rye Brook, NY: Peter Pauper Press).

2 Dr. Myles Munroe, The Principles and Power of Vision: Keys to Achieving Personal and Corporate Destiny, (New Kensington, PA: Whitaker House, 2006).

3 Robert Moss, "How Bottled Water Became America's Most Popular Beverage," Serious Eats, Updated March 7, 2023. Retrieved from https://www.seriouseats.com/how-bottled-water-became-americas-most-popular-beverage

4 "Sales Volume of Bottled Water in the United States from 2011 to 2022," Statista, May 2023, Retrieved from https://www.statista.com/statistics/237832/volume-of-bottled-water-in-the-us/#:~:text=In%202022%2C%2015.9%20billion%20gallons,considerably%20with%20each%20consecutive%20year.

5 Carol Tucker, "The 1950s – Powerful Years for Religion." USC Today, June 16, 1997, Retrieved from https://today.usc.edu/The-1950s-Powerful-Years-for-Religion/#:~:text=Churches%20and%20schools%20were%20being,highest%20percentage%20in%20U.S.%20history

6 *God's Big Idea: Reclaiming God's Original Purpose for Your Life* by Myles Munroe, Destiny Image, 2008.

7 A.W. Tozer, The Knowledge of the Holy, (New York: HarperOne, 2009).

8 Jack Hayford, "The Power of Words," Jack Hayford Ministries, 2011. Retrieved from https://www.jackhayford.org/teaching/articles/the-power-of-words/

9 Hannah Ritchie, Pablo Rosado and Max Roser (2019) - "Access to Energy" Published online at OurWorldInData.org. Retrieved from: 'https://ourworldindata.org/energy-access' [Online Resource]

10 Merriam-Webster.com Dictionary, s.v. "government," accessed April 30, 2024, https://www.merriam-webster.com/dictionary/government.

11 "Cosmetic Surgery & Skincare," published online by Cleveland Clinic. Updated on March, 6, 2024, Retrieved from: https://my.clevelandclinic.org/health/procedures/11007-cosmetic-surgery, [Online Resource]

12 "About Three-in-Ten U.S. Adults are Now Religiously Unaffiliated," Report published by Pew Research Center, December 14, 2021, Retrieved from https://www.pewresearch.org/religion/2021/12/14/about-three-in-ten-u-s-adults-are-now-religiously-unaffiliated/

13 Leo Tolstoy, quoted by AZ Quotes, Retrieved on https://www.azquotes.com/quote/941535